EARLY GREEK LAWGIVERS

Classical World Series

Classical World Series

EARLY GREEK LAWGIVERS

John David Lewis

Bristol Classical Press

First published in 2007 by
Bristol Classical Press
an imprint of
Gerald Duckworth & Co. Ltd.
90-93 Cowcross Street, London EC1M 6BF
Tel: 020 7490 7300
Fax: 020 7490 0080
inquiries@duckworth-publishers.co.uk
www.ducknet.co.uk

A catalogue record for this book is available
from the British Library

ISBN 978 1 85399 697 9

Cover: drawing of Solon by Kimothy Piorkowsky.

Typeset by Ray Davies
Printed and bound in Great Britain by
CPI Antony Rowe, Chippenham

Contents

List of Illustrations

Preface

The purpose of this book is to examine the early Greek lawgivers with reference to the epigraphic and literary evidence by which we know them. The first three chapters offer a very short introduction to the history of early Greek law, including its sources and a few general problems. The next four chapters are focused on the lawgivers themselves. A chronological table is included at the front, and the text is followed by questions for further study and a glossary of transliterated terms.

I have benefited enormously from a grant by the Anthem Foundation for Objectivist Studies. In addition, Professor Fred Miller, and everyone else at the Social Philosophy and Policy Center of Bowling Green State University, provided a Visiting Fellowship and a friendly, collegial environment. Jeff Pinkham read a draft with an active pen in hand. Duckworth's ace editor, Deborah Blake, and two anonymous readers kept me in tune with English spellings. Thanks beyond thanks go to my wife Casey; my *sine qua non* in every respect.

J.D.L.

Chronological Table of Events, Lawgivers and Sources

Many of these dates are traditional, and at best approximate. It is particularly difficult to establish dates for persons who are semi-mythological and buried in the mists of time. The dates are intended to offer a relative chronology based on approximate time of flourishing, rather than precise and absolute figures.

Near Eastern, Cretan, and Mycenaean Greek civilizations up to *c.* 1150 BC		
Dates	**Periods and events**	**People and sources**
1750 BC		Hammurabi's Law Code of Babylonia.
1900-1200 BC	Minoan Crete.	Minos, and Rhadamanthus.
1200	Trojan War.	
1500-1150	Mycenaean Greece.	

The Greek Dark Ages and Heroic Age *c.* 1150-750 BC		
900-750		Homer's *Iliad* and *Odyssey* composed.
750		Hesiod's *Theogony* and *Works and Days* composed.

The Archaic period *c.* 750 BC to the Persian invasions		
729	Founding of Catana.	
700		Theseus unifies Athens (?).
685	Founding of Chalcedon.	
650	Founding of Locri Epizephyrii.	
650	Law inscription of Dreros.	Tyrtaeus (poet). Lycurgus, lawgiver of Sparta (?). Zaleucus, lawgiver of Locri Epizephyrii.
621		Drakon writes laws in Athens.
620		Epimenides of Crete purifies Athens. Charondas, lawgiver of Catana.

Dates	Periods and events	People and sources
600		Pittacus, tyrant of Mytilene.
750-500	Lyric poets flourish.	Xenophanes (poet). Theognis (poet). Alcaeus (poet). Archilochus (poet).
594		Solon is Chief Archon of Athens.
575-550	Law inscription of Chios.	Croesus of Lydia meets Solon (?).
550-525	Law inscription of Eretria.	

The Classical period
from the Persian invasions to the death of Alexander

490-479	Two Persian invasions of Greece.	
450	Law Code of Gortyn.	
450		Hippodamus of Miletus designs Athens' new port, the Peiraeus.
440		Herodotus writes the *Histories*.
431-404	Peloponnesian War (Athens and Sparta).	
409	Draco's Law is re-inscribed.	
360-322		Demosthenes flourishes.
340		Plato writes the *Laws*.
330		Aristotle writes the *Politics*, and the *Constitution of the Athenians*.
323	Death of Alexander the Great.	

The Hellenistic and Roman periods

50 BC		Cicero writes *On Laws*.
late first century BC		Dionysius of Halicarnassus writes *Roman Antiquities*. Diodorus of Sicily writes *History*. Livy writes *History*.
AD 100		Plutarch writes *Lives*.
AD 220		Diogenes Laertius writes *Lives of the Philosophers*. Aelian writes *Varia Historia*.
AD 450		John of Stobi writes *Selections* and *Anthology*.

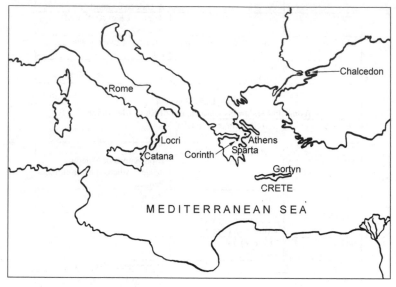

Fig. 1. Map of the Mediterranean with major locations cited in the text.

Chapter 1

Approaching Greek Laws and Lawgivers

At the start of Plato's *Laws,* the fourth-century philosopher's last work, three men are walking towards Mount Ida, the traditional birthplace of Zeus on Crete. They are discussing how to design the best laws possible for a new city, the fictional Magnesia. On the one hand, they had largely a free hand; they could start from scratch, and write whatever laws they thought appropriate. They had no need either to obey their ancient traditions in detail, or to remain tied to present laws. Yet neither could they break completely away from those traditions, or from the ancestral laws derived from them – such customs were key to understanding what the laws should be, and to grasping what people in their own day would be willing to accept. The ancient origins of Crete's laws could not be cavalierly dismissed.

The stranger from Athens asks his two companions:

'Tell me, kind sirs, who is it that you honour with having established your laws? Is it a god, or a man?'

Clinias, the Cretan, answers:

'A god, my good man, for sure. We Cretans say it is Zeus; on Sparta – the home of my friend here – they say it is Apollo. Is that right?'
(Plato *Laws* 1, 624Af.)

The people of Crete, the Athenian Stranger continues, must have followed the stories left by the epic poet Homer, whose verses sang the praises of the ancient Cretan King Minos, and who connected the king to the earliest Greek gods and heroes. Minos, the stories say, had consulted with his father Zeus for the laws, and brought them to the Cretans – as, deep in the past, Apollo had once favoured Sparta, and Athena had protected Athens. It is surely important that Plato's conversants are walking towards a sacred site, for they too connect the ancient laws to a divine origin, and are looking to a divine source for the inspiration and the legitimacy needed to create their own laws.

But, Clinias adds, there was another influence on the early Cretans. Rhadamanthus, the brother of Minos, who flourished perhaps a thousand years earlier, had enjoyed a soaring reputation for fairness in resolving disputes. He had brought justice to people in a direct and concrete way, by resolving their conflicts in a way that lessened the possibility of vengeance and violence. This was as important to the people of Crete as the laws themselves, for it showed them how justice could be practised in their own lives. Minos enacted *themistes* – commands or statutes that had the force of a king's power, and which were imposed on the Cretans – while Rhadamanthus brought a sense of fairness and justice (*dikê*) to the resolution of their particular problems.

There was, according to these legends, a dual source in the ancient past for the Cretan political and legal order, which has come not only from the direct intervention of a god, whose spokesman writes a comprehensive code of laws, but also from a human figure, renowned for his justice, who brought order, stability and justice through fair mediation of disputes. Combining the actions of Minos and Rhadamanthus, what emerges is the figure of the lawgiver, the legislator who brings laws to his people, and orders their world so that they may live together justly.

Neither Minos nor Rhadamanthus can be confirmed as an historical person; each may represent centuries of stories, spanning cultural, social and political developments across generations, but solidifying over time into the figures revealed by the oral and written traditions. There were many variations among such traditions – the Cretans, Spartans, Athenians and others posited different lawgivers and gods at the foundations of their cities – but in each case the figure of the ancient lawgiver occupied a central place in Greek views of wisdom, justice, order, goodness and law. He was among the most respected of men, a bringer of laws and of justice whose reputation as a moral authority grew as generations passed by. Man without justice, wrote Aristotle, is the basest of beings; it is the lawgiver who brings a sense of justice to his *polis*, and allows his fellows to live a fully human life (Aristotle *Politics* 1.2).

Many lawgivers were real historical persons – and they did bring laws and constitutions to their cities – but they have also become figures shaped by centuries of legends. To delve into the lives and work of the lawgivers is to partake of the myths and stories that served as historical anchors for the early Greek cities, and that have moulded our view of them. These stories, preserved in a literary tradition, are portals into how the Greeks viewed the foundations of their lives, including the norms and values they associated with their past, and used to guide their present.

Given this myth-historical background, it should not be surprising that the Greeks did not approach their legal history – or their laws – as we would today. Plato's characters do not turn to legal textbooks, libraries of statutes or systematized precedents akin to the later Roman law-codes in order to determine the position of a particular law in a wider scheme of organization. In general terms, most Greeks were less concerned about writing statutes than about making certain that a sense of justice was maintained in the judgement of individual cases. To determine the meaning of this justice, the philosopher Plato focused primarily on the moral character of the city, as founded on the character of its citizens. Most lawgivers also recognized that the goodness of a community was vitally dependent upon the goodness of the people in it, who must be able to express their views, argue their positions and pursue their own aims without an oppressive authority over them. The Greeks needed to maintain order in their cities, but not at the price of tyranny; as time passed, they developed forums in which to argue their cases openly, and (in many cases) they wrote laws to guide the decisions of those forums. This was what Minos represents: the creation of laws, publicly displayed and openly argued, to prevent the outrages of improper judgements.

Modern scholars have wrestled to understand early Greek laws and lawgivers in terms that do not distort the Greek views. Some scholars have adopted functionalist or evolutionary perspectives on early Greek law; some have approached the topic as historians, cultural anthropologists, or legal analysts, by calling on natural or positivistic legal theories. It can be tempting to interpret Greek laws and institutions using modern standards of judicial authority, courtroom procedures, legal scholarship and rules of evidence, and then to apply those same interpretations into even earlier, pre-classical developments. Such anachronisms must be resisted.

Poets such as Homer and Hesiod were singing their works at the time when the *polis* – the Greek city-state, of which hundreds appeared across the Mediterranean world – was rising as a political form. Each of these towns – each *polis* – was politically and legally independent and self-governing, beholden to no larger empire and answerable to no one outside itself. Each made its own laws, enforced them by its own standards and system of justice, and selected officials by the means it thought appropriate. As a result, the laws and courts of the Greeks remained, in a specific sense, primitive. This does not mean unsophisticated or simple. It does mean that they seldom had to apply their laws beyond their own *polis*, and could therefore rely upon many unwritten customs that everyone knew by virtue of living there.

'Greek law' is a wide perspective on the disparate 'laws' used to bring order to individual *poleis*. When we speak of 'Greek law' or a 'Greek lawgiver', we must ask which set of laws or which lawgiver we are considering for which particular *polis*, for there were no universal Greek institutions to enact and enforce Greek laws across a singular Greek world. The sense of justice and of laws was unified *within* each *polis*, but there was no 'law' common to all the Greeks beyond the desire for independence, deference to the gods, and language (which itself had many variations in dialect). Consequently, there is no singular 'Greek law' apart from the particular laws in each *polis*, and no Greek 'lawgiver' but rather 'lawgivers'.

In his own *polis,* a Greek could take for granted many of the rules and procedures that need to be minutely spelled out today. Many of those customs remain difficult for us to grasp, if not completely hidden – especially for a time as far back as the pre-classical, archaic period of Greek history, when the early lawgivers lived. The harsh murder laws of Draco of Athens, for instance, may have reflected widely-accepted customs in Athens during a social crisis. Solon of Athens may have set out to correct the injustices that had arisen in the past generation; perhaps by returning Athens to certain earlier standards of propriety, while enacting reforms that would change Athens fundamentally. Other lawgivers might have promulgated specific social and educational practices that reinforced existing ideas; Lycurgus of Sparta may exemplify this. Other might have brought in laws that had been used elsewhere, as the laws of Charondas of Catana may have spread through Sicily and southern Italy.

Our use of translations can bring additional problems. If we translate the Greek word *nomos* as 'law', do we mean an 'Act' that has been passed by the Greek equivalent of a 'Parliament' (or 'Congress'), signed by the 'Prime Minister' (or 'President') with the approval of the 'Queen', which is then examined through various 'courts' before facing a 'constitutional' challenge before the 'House of Lords' (or the 'Supreme Court')? Or do we mean a general maxim or rule for living, powerful but unspecific, with moral as well as legal connotations? Or is *nomos* rather the idea of 'law' in the general sense that underlies particular laws? In different contexts, *nomos* can mean 'norm' or 'custom' as well as 'law', and it is not always easy to distinguish a Greek norm from a law. Given these wide and narrow senses of *nomos*, and the changes in its connotations over history, how then would *nomos* relate to words such as *themis* ('order'), *psêphisma* ('decree'), *dikê* ('justice'), or *themistes* ('statutes')? These are difficult problems.

To take another example, when we read Aristotle's conclusion that the Athenian lawgiver Solon established a '*politeia*' for Athens, and we translate this as 'constitution', we run the risk of conflating Aristotle's sense of *politeia* (the 'organization' of the *polis*, including its distribution of offices) into a modern 'constitution'. It would surely be wrong to see Solon of Athens as some kind of modern political theorist or constitutional scholar. But the problem goes back even further, for neither did Solon – in the early sixth century BC – understand his *politeia* as Aristotle did in the fourth century BC. Solon did bring reforms to Athens, and what resulted was a *polis* with a certain organization, but Solon never called a constitutional convention to establish new institutions, nor did he consider the various forms of *poleis* analytically (as did Aristotle). He rather used poetry to inculcate certain habits of mind, connected to social rituals as well as to reforms of offices, by which he could bring his sense of justice to Athens. It is the lawgiver's focus on these virtues and habits – and his writing of laws in order to translate the norms into particular cases – that allows him to bring order to his *polis*, and allows his fellows to accept and follow his written laws.

Rather than our seeing the laws, the magistrates, and the courts as applying standards of justice that are cast in the form of organized laws, to be understood from the perspectives of modern legal theory, it may be more productive to see them as creating a forum in which disputes can be publicly aired without violence. The Greeks had an *agonistic* culture, in which competition and struggle were omnipresent. Many scholars have come to recognize that Greek laws, and their practice, must be seen as part of this culture of contestation. The Greeks might not have thought of their courts as places to resolve disputes, but perhaps as forums to continue them, albeit it in ways that did not destroy the order and prosperity in their cities. In any event, Greek laws – rules which served to regularize the deliberations and decisions of the courts and magistrates – cannot be understood without considering the deeper cultural, political and moral norms of Greek political life. Similarly, the figure of the lawgiver – the point of focus for the birth of a stable, just order in the *polis* – reflects the underlying values of the *polis*, all the while shaping those values through his laws and judgements.

Epigraphic sources for early Greek laws

Epigraphy (*epi* 'upon' plus *graphê* 'depiction') is the study of stone inscriptions. When the Greeks wrote laws, both early in the archaic period and in later times, they carved them into stone or wood, and set them up for public viewing. Such stones have been found in many places, across centuries, and they indicate a certain openness in their societies, a willingness to deliberate important issues publicly, rather than to impose the decision of a monarch. Yet such a stone implies that there were limits established for all such decisions, and that even those who claimed popular support for their positions could not act without constraints. Because a stone is direct evidence from the time in which it was written, it has a solidity that we cannot take for granted in a literary work, which has been copied multiple times, and which may be more a product of a literary tradition than direct evidence from the time it discusses.

If we want to read Greek laws that are indisputably real, we need to read inscriptions. But they come with their own problems. The evidence they provide is found on shattered fragments of stone, and is too incomplete to allow us to write a narrative history of the past. They are likely divorced from the political and physical context in which they were written, and may not reveal the supporting information by which they were understood. Who wrote them, when and under what circumstances is frustratingly difficult to determine – and may be impossible to know with certainty. For such questions we must call upon surrounding archaeology, similar artifacts in other areas, and literary texts.

One problem of interpretation concerns the purpose of such laws. This was, given our evidence, probably not to provide a comprehensive, systematic record of all the laws, but rather to provide a stable point of reference for issues that may have been in dispute. For instance, a constitutional law – which deals with political institutions or offices – may not tell us the basic organization of *polis* institutions, either because this was common knowledge for everyone in that *polis*, or because the stone with that information was lost. The law's concern might rather have been with setting term limits for the offices, a point of contention because some improperly ambitious men had tried to hold those offices indefinitely. The law could have been in reaction to a growing threat of tyranny. Similarly, a religious law will likely not provide us with the details of the rituals practised at the time – which were well-known – but would have addressed only issues that were in dispute or needed clarification. A murder law, to take another example, can tell us only certain very broad aspects of the response that would have followed a homicide.

An inscription from the island of Chios, dated to 575-550 BC, is a constitutional law (M&L no. 8). The stone, all though highly fragmented and beyond definitive translation, tells us that the *demos* (the people), assembled in council, and with the power to inflict penalties, issued *rhêtrai* (decisions of some kind), which defined the actions that officials could take, required those officials to protect the laws of the *polis*, held them accountable for bribes, and allowed an appeal either to the people (the *demos*) or to a council. Those hearing such appeals had to take an oath to follow the laws. We may infer from this that there were problems on Chios with some people trying to hold power beyond proper limits, and that 'the people' (who were they?) were unhappy with many of the decisions of their judges. They asserted their influence through their assemblies. The result was some kind of differentiation of the powers of the various officials, the council, and the people, and perhaps an early 'checks and balances' between them.

Some of the issues here – particularly those concerned with judicial procedure – were also addressed in an inscription from Eretria, a *polis* on the island of Euboea, dating to *c.* 550-525 BC (Gagarin, *Early Greek Law,* 91-3). It states that justice is to be done (meaning, decisions made) only after oaths have been taken, and it sets a schedule for the payment of fines with penalties for failure to comply. Such inscriptions suggest attempts to restrain the power of some men, by establishing defined procedures by which they can be held accountable, or by specifying how they should make judgements. As in the Chios inscription, there is no lawgiver mentioned by name, but there is a clear attempt to bring political matters under public control.

In the late fifth century the people of Athens were concerned to maintain the stability of their *polis*, so they appointed officials – *nomothetai* – to reinscribe their ancestral laws, which harked back to their early lawgivers. One such reinscription of 409/8 BC preserved a homicide law attributed to the early lawgiver Draco (*c.* 621 BC) – the only early homicide law known in any detail (M&L no. 86, translated in part in Chapter 6 below). The inscription is a product of the late fifth century BC and reflects the memory that the people of the time had of Draco's law from some 200 years earlier.

Many questions of interpretation follow. Are such inscriptions an accurate reconstruction of the ancestral laws, taken from evidence now lost? Or are they loose approximations, based on the state of memory at the time? Or are they rather attempts to use the prestige of the ancient laws in order to legitimate and solidify the practices of a later time? In other words, is the inscription of 409/8 BC, for instance, primary evidence about laws that were over two centuries old when it was carved, or is it secondary evidence from the later time? The particular stones of 409/8 are without doubt direct evidence from the late fifth century, and their relationship to the earlier laws is subject to interpretation, which will depend largely upon whether we have other information against which to verify and interpret the law and its historical context. Draco's law, as understood by the people of late fifth-century Athens, may or may not have been historically accurate – but it served their purposes, by solidifying, into stone, the consequences of murder, in terms that held deep cultural significance.

Fig. 2. Draco's law on homicide, reinscribed 409/8 BC. Epigraphical Museum, Athens, no. 6602 (*IG* I³ 104).

Inscriptions from Crete

Some of the oldest and most complete Greek legal inscriptions still extant come from Crete, an island with many different customs, communities and political systems. The oldest inscribed law that we have is from the otherwise unremarkable town of Dreros, *c*. 650 BC. As translated by epigraphers Meiggs and Lewis, it reads:

The *polis* has thus decided; when a man has been *kosmos*, the same man shall not be *kosmos* again for ten years. If he does act as *kosmos*, whatever judgements he gives, he shall owe double, and he shall lose his rights to office, as long as he lives, and whatever he does as *kosmos* shall be nothing (M&L no. 2)

This is a constitutional law, which set term limits for officials, with penalties for violating those limits. The *polis* here is, in some way, a gathering of the citizens or their leaders, although the criteria for being a citizen and what constitutes a decision by the *polis* remain unclear to us. A *kosmos* is an official with certain powers, limited to one term of one year in any ten-year period. The Greek term *kosmos*, used more widely, indicates an orderly or systematic arrangement of something, such as the heavens, or the soldiers in Homer's *Iliad*. Used as an official title here, it suggests political order in the *polis* – of what kind we do not know – that is being maintained by chosen officials.

As for all such laws, there is a penalty involved for breaking it; should a man declare himself a *kosmos* in an impermissible way, or accept an improper acclamation of *kosmos* by his supporters, then he shall owe fines and forfeit his right to future office, and his decisions shall be invalid. The law goes on to require oaths by officials or perhaps a body of officials, although the nature of the oaths and the identities of the officials remain unclear. The *kosmos* may have had other duties, but the only one discussed here is that of hearing cases. Either we have lost the laws pertaining to those other duties, or only the matter of his judging cases required a law – or there is a different explanation. In any case, the *polis* is asserting itself as an authority higher than particular officials. This implies that someone is making laws, in a public context or at least in the name of the entire *polis*, which everyone must follow – even the officials themselves.

The longest extant Greek legal inscriptions are from the town of Gortyn in central southern Crete. The so-called 'Great Code', dating from the fifth century BC, consists of twelve stone columns bearing in all about 600 lines. It deals primarily with family relations and inheritances, only slightly with contracts or non-family property, and describes nothing akin to criminal law. Its massive size makes it unique among our evidence, but even so it is incomplete and leaves many questions open. There is no literary material to judge these carvings against; the Cretans are otherwise silent about how their laws would relate to their communities.

We cannot easily use the laws of Gortyn or Dreros as exemplars of laws across Crete, any more than the laws of Athens represent the laws of all *poleis* on mainland Greece – or the laws of the United Kingdom today represent laws across the English-speaking world. Nor can we assume that the law is consistent with another time, centuries removed. But such laws do demonstrate the sweeping importance of rules that are written and in public view. The stability provided by such an inscription, carved into the heart of a city's life, is connected to the growth of law itself, as a solid set of norms that exists independent of anyone's memory or manipulation. Despite many problems of context and interpretation, such inscriptions remain our most direct and solid portal into early Greek laws.

Fig. 3. The Gortyn law code, section of column 1. Author's drawing from a photograph.

Literary sources and lawgiver legends

Inscriptions are indisputably real, but they offer us little or no elaboration of what their laws meant to observers or how they were applied, and they provide almost no information about the early lawgivers themselves. To fill in these areas we need literary texts, which are lush in their descriptions, but have come to us through centuries of editing, copying, interpretation and emendation. They constitute a literary tradition that tells us what later Greeks thought *about* the lawgivers; but apart from preserved poetic verses, they are not primary evidence *from* the lawgivers. The inscriptions are rock-solid but cryptic; the literary texts are elaborate but fluid.

Solon, the lawgiver of Athens, is a case in point. Our only primary evidence for the conditions in early sixth-century Athens remains the fragments of his verses, preserved in later writers. But even a cursory reading of those fragments demonstrates their lack of 'legal' and 'constitutional' concerns. Rather than laws, they leave us maxims of wisdom, justice and fate, concerned with excellence and the virtues required for the good life. Solon, along with other archaic poets such as Archilochus, Tyrtaeus, Xenophanes and Theognis, is thus known as a 'wisdom poet'. Yet the later prose writers who preserved this poetry may not have had accurate information, and must have selected these verses for their own purposes. In the process of preserving Solon's memory – and the laws associated with him – Herodotus, Plato, Aristotle, Demosthenes, Plutarch and others also shaped that memory, adding to his renown, reinterpreting or even inventing events associated with him, turning Solon the historical man into Solon the lawgiver of legend.

A place to begin the search for memory of Solon is in *Histories* of Herodotus, written around 440 BC (1.30-2). Herodotus is concerned with the deep cultural background to the Greco-Persian Wars of 490 and 480/79 BC, and he interprets the past in terms familiar to him and his audience. Writing some 120 to 160 years after Solon lived, Herodotus places him with the Lydian King Croesus, nearly 50 years after Solon first held office, in order to illustrate something of the character of the eastern king, his attitude towards wealth, and the reasons why he was conquered by the Persians. This moral lesson that concerned Herodotus – embodied in Solon – centres on the nature of fate, justice, and blessedness, all of which are central motifs to Herodotus. 'Solon' is here a man of wisdom, or a religious sage.

The treatment by Herodotus may be compared to Solon's own poem 13, which presents Solon's views of *moira* ('allotted portion', or 'dispensation of the gods') in relation to justice and wealth. Herodotus has adapted the tales surrounding Solon to his own purposes, using him to illustrate a moral point in his story, and perhaps at the cost of historical accuracy. The Herodotean Solon, for instance, expresses the idea that 'no man can be judged blessed before his death', an idea that is not found in Solon's preserved poems. Herodotus shapes our own view of Solon, all the while demonstrating how he was used by later writers as a figure of moral excellence, for an audience that would understand such a lesson in their own terms.

Solon's poem 13 is actually preserved in the works of John of Stobi, or John Stobaeus, a compiler of the fifth century AD, who preserved excerpts from many writers, but about whom little is known. This adds another level to the process of literary selection, preservation and transmission – and makes it all the harder for us to discern Solon's original purpose in writing his poem.

The legal and political orators from fourth-century Athens had a different purpose: to win an argument and a lawsuit. They use the ancient lawgivers, especially Solon of Athens, as legal and moral authorities, calling on the moral force of Solon's name in order to gain the votes of a jury. A speech attributed to the fourth-century orator Demosthenes, but probably written by someone else, cites a law of inheritance that he links to Solon:

> Any citizen of the *polis*, with the exception of those adopted when Solon entered office, and who then becomes unable either to renounce or to claim his inheritance, shall have the right to dispose of his property by a will as he wishes, if he has no legitimate male heirs, unless his mind is impaired by madness, old age, drugs or disease, or he is under the influence of a woman, or under constraint of necessity or deprived of his freedom. (Demosthenes, *Against Stephanus II*, 14)

Demosthenes here claims an ancient standing for this law by calling upon the revered name of Solon, and connecting the law back to him. This adds a powerful sense of legitimacy to Demosthenes' speech, but it does nothing to tell us whether Solon actually made such a law. (Nor does it tell us whether Demosthenes deserves to prevail over his opponent.) 'Solon' has here become a legal witness and authority – some 200 years after his death.

Sometimes an orator's use of the ancient lawgiver flies in the face of his own argument, as when Demosthenes, in his speech *On the False Legation*, section 255, quotes from a poem by Solon. Yet Demosthenes' lead-in to this poem illustrates, by way of analogy to sculpture, one of the problems involved in inferring the status of an earlier figure from later evidence. Demosthenes accuses his opponent Aeschines of claiming that a statue of Solon at Salamis, in which Solon has his hand wrapped into his tunic, illustrates the self-restraint of the earlier orators. Aeschines has implied that Demosthenes is immoderate in his bearing, and thus flawed when compared to Solon. But Demosthenes goes on to say that the statue is less than 50 years old. The sculptor could not have known what Solon looked like, or how he held his hands. By analogy, Aeschines' reference to 'Solon' is flawed. The lesson is that all later material – such as Demosthenes' own speech, or even the presence of the Solon poem in the speech, which may have been inserted by a later editor – is at centuries' remove from the earlier time, and must be understood with reference to its own purpose.

Also from the fourth century are the discussions of Solon and other wisdom poets and lawgivers by philosophers such as Plato and Aristotle. The serious way they call upon Solon and others is evidence for the deep importance of the lawgiver traditions. But their writings are complex, used to support their philosophical purposes, and framed in terms that are highly anachronistic to the earlier period. Plato, for instance, in his dialogue the *Timaeus*, cites Solon as having brought norms, customs and laws to Athens from Egypt (21A-26D). Plato is centrally concerned with the habits of mind and character that influence present-day conditions, and he uses Solon as a point of focus for his own purposes. 'Solon' here is a sage, used to bring eastern customs to Greece and to illustrate issues of cosmology, knowledge and ethics, as well as law.

Fig. 4. The Aristotelian *Constitution of the Athenians*. Papyrus (London: British Museum, 1891), col. 11.

Aristotle's *Politics*, especially Book 2, illuminates the lawgivers in terms appropriate to Aristotle's political philosophy, using them to exemplify various types of political systems. The Aristotelian *Constitution of the Athenians* preserves substantial material from and about Solon, including his crucially important poem 36 (in section 12) which connects freedom, justice and force to written laws that are applied 'similarly' to people of every status. Yet Aristotle's discussion uses political terms – such as *dêmokratia*, 'democracy' – that are not found in evidence from Solon's own time. Aristotle also analyses these social issues in terms of rich versus poor; he presents Solon as establishing jury courts, revising coinage exchange rates, etc. – ideas and institutions that are anachronistic to Solon's own time, and yet remain important to Aristotle's purposes. 'Solon' becomes a politician who would have been at home in the fourth century.

The later flow of the historical tradition may be read in Diodorus of Sicily, an historian of the first century BC, who wrote a universal history in Greek while living under Roman rule. He embellishes and transmits information from earlier historians, especially Ephorus, who are otherwise lost to us. Diodorus, for instance, attributes to Solon the idea that athletes contribute nothing to the security of their cities, but that only men of wisdom and excellence are able to ward off danger (9.2.5). This idea is also found in a poem by the archaic poet Xenophanes, although missing in Solon. 'Solon' in Diodorus has been made inseparable from a tradition of ancient thinkers.

The early third-century AD biographer Diogenes Laertius placed Solon with other important thinkers – but much of his account is anecdotal and not reliable. He expresses what was known – or invented – in his own time. The epitome of the Greek and Roman biographical tradition came earlier, in Plutarch, who wrote at the end of the first and start of the second centuries AD. Plutarch writes the lives of Theseus, Lycurgus, Solon and others, evaluating them according to his own Platonic philosophy, with a view to reconstructing their moral characters rather than details of events. This leads to many problems of interpretation. Plutarch, for instance, places Solon amorously with the tyrant Pisistratus of Athens, perhaps in the late 560s BC. But this too is chronologically difficult, given that Solon was made chief archon, or official, of Athens in 594 BC – a conclusion supported by multiple later sources. If Solon was with Pisistratus, he was either advanced in years at the time of his alleged love affair, or extraordinarily young when he became archon. Scholars have come up with various theories to explain this chronology; in the end, it remains impossible to verify.

Rather than trying to reconcile the accounts of disparate authors, a better approach may be to recognize that Plutarch – like all of these writers – has used Solon for his own purposes. Plutarch is clear, at the start of his *Life of Alexander*, that he does not intend to write histories, but rather lives. 'If I do not record the most illustrious deeds of these men or describe them comprehensively', he writes, 'please do not judge this as a fault. I am writing biography, not history.' This is concerned with the virtues and vices of the men involved, not the details of their most brilliant exploits. Seemingly minor remarks or incidents, Plutarch states, may reveal more about these matters of character than do the grand battles and political intrigues that occupy the historian.

Plutarch's *Life of Solon*, then, is not a comprehensive historical account of the lawgiver's actions, but a presentation of Solon's character according to Plutarch's moral ideas. That does not mean the account is invalid – the moral aspects of a lawgiver's program may reach most deeply into the nature of the values in his own time – but it does mean that we must evaluate Plutarch's work with due recognition of this purpose. Once we do so – and should we try to reconcile the accounts of the various sources – we may find that the details of Solon's life that we have are as much the product of a tradition as they are an accurate representation of the past. What we have here is a 'legendary lawgiver' – a man whose work has taken on a significance that reaches across centuries.

Chapter 2

Early Greek Order, Justice and Law

A full description of Greek law and its history is far beyond the scope of this book. But a few basic issues in its development are needed for even a short presentation of the lawgivers, their deeds and their reputations.

Mediation and arbitration in Homer

The early poet Homer, in his *Iliad* and *Odyssey*, presents a world in which aristocratic warrior-heroes – each with his contingent of mostly unnamed followers – make all major decisions and dominate the action. There are assemblies of the soldiers, and their enthusiasm for the war is vital to its success, but as the common soldier Thersites ('the worst of the Achaians') found out, it is not the place of the rank and file to deliberate with the commanders or to question their decisions (*Iliad* 2.211-77). When, in the *Odyssey*, suitors from the surrounding area encroach upon Odysseus' prerogatives by moving into his home, he slaughters them brutally, and without deference to any other authority. These leaders have an elevated, in some cases semi-divine, status, and they hold the staff or sceptre of command over the nameless, unranked soldiers.

Yet the commanders can dispute with one another, placing everyone in danger. To avoid bloodshed they may try to come to terms with one another by negotiation, wagers, oaths or compromises. Their disputes may be resolved – or an attempt made to resolve them, at least – through a mediator, a third-party who stands between the disputants and tries to reduce the tension by bringing them to some kind of agreement. When, at the start of the *Iliad*, Agamemnon and Achilles fall into conflict over certain spoils of war, Nestor attempts to mediate. As Achilles dashes the staff of command to the ground, and Agamemnon continues to rage, Nestor stands in the middle between them, 'in good intention towards the both of them':

> and between them rose Nestor,
> the fair-speaker of Pylos, from whose tongue
> stream words sweeter than honey (*Iliad* 1.247-9)

This is mediation because it is up to the parties to agree or not with Nestor's decision; they are not compelled to do so. Nestor enjoins them both to 'be persuaded'; 'obey the both of you' he says, 'since to be persuaded is better' than to continue the fight. Such a mediator has no power to enforce his decision, and the parties are under no obligation to act as he suggests. Agamemnon refuses, blaming Achilles, who responds with his own angry rejoinder. Until they agree otherwise, the confrontation will continue, and may become a feud. It is of great importance that there is no king here dictating and enforcing a decision, no fixed institutions to bring their dispute before, and no body of written laws to consult. The men must agree upon a solution, or the dispute will continue.

The mediator is a man who stands not with either of the two sides, but rather as an independent man of the middle, who calls upon accepted standards of fairness to bring a solution acceptable to all parties. His interest (at least ideally) is to see the dispute resolved, not to see either side's position upheld. In the centuries after Homer, the archaic lawgivers Solon of Athens, Lycurgus of Sparta and Charondas of Catana would fulfil such a role, as men of the 'middle citizens', because they had neither the interests of the rich nor those of the poor at heart (Aristotle, *Politics* 4.11-12). The middle position economically – for a man of moderate means – may be distinguished from a position based on birth; at the start of his biography of Solon, Plutarch refers to Solon as of moderate wealth and power, but descended from a noble family. He is credited with having the intelligence and virtues of a noble-born citizen, although rich neither in money nor in political power.

Mediation can be contrasted with arbitration, in which the disputants select a third party to bring a decision, and they agree to follow that decision, whatever it may be. The importance of the agreement can be underscored by an oath – a promise to act as they have agreed – and by a wager – something material that adds value to the promise. An example here is in the dispute that arose in the *Iliad* during the chariot race in the funeral games: Idomeneus claims that Diomedes is in the lead; Ajax son of Oileus favours Eumelos. Idomeneus asks Ajax to accept a wager, or a bet, and to call on an arbitrator to resolve the dispute:

> let us wager a cauldron or a tripod
> and make Agamemnon son of Atreus the *histor*
> of which horses are leading, so that you'll learn and pay
> (Iliad 23.485-7)

The *histor* is here an arbitrator or a judge, but more fundamentally an investigator, or one who knows. (His product, or account, is *historia*.) He is selected for his intelligence as well as his fairness. In this case, the wager – should Ajax accept it – would take the form of a binding oath and a prize for the winner. Both sides would have to accept Agamemnon's decision, lest they break the oath and invite divine destruction and a massive reaction from their fellows. Ajax refuses the wager – perhaps he knows how weak his claim is – thus ending the dispute. In a legal context, the refusal of one party to take an oath could be taken to mean that he has no defensible case. In either event, the parties negotiate over whether they wish to engage in a wager, and whom they should invite in to render a decision.

In Homer's world such mediation, arbitration, oaths, and wagers are always informal, even if highly ritualistic and taken very seriously. There are strong customs and a sense of honour, but no institutions or fixed procedures, and no written laws or jurors sworn to uphold them. To take one example, strange to modern ears, murder does not require common action akin to public prosecution; unless the violence threatens to spread, the matter is a concern only to the families or friends of those involved. The exception would be feuds involving powerful figures, whose contention could lead to wider strife. In the end, self-help – each person's assertion of his own prerogatives – generally took the place of formal legal and political institutions. The mediator, or arbitrator, was a man of wisdom, but he had only his own wits to call on for a decision, and no power to enforce it.

Order, justice and law in Homer and Hesiod

Despite the informal nature of these incidents, Homer's world is not one of anarchic violence. Strong customs and moral norms have been established over human life, which limit the scope of actions available to the heroes and define the terms of their honour and renown. In the *Odyssey*, Homer described a sense of law as the basic difference between human beings and beasts. The Cyclopes were 'lawless beasts' (*athemistoi*), who neither till the soil nor plant crops; the earth brings all they need without effort. Nor do they have any place of public assembly, nor laws held in common; each is a law unto himself and his family, and with no regard for his neighbours (*Odyssey* 9.105-15). They have no *themis*, or order, governing their community – they have no community! – and thus no common *themistes,* or statutes, created in cooperation with others. Each rather makes his own decrees for himself and his family.

Themis, related to the verb *tithêmi*, to 'place' or 'set,' is the general sense of order that is established, or set, by the gods over human life. This order is as much religious as it is political or legal; such distinctions had not yet been made. More narrowly, *themistes*, 'statutes', are the particular decrees established, enacted, or decreed by kings and legitimate rulers. Without such a wide sense of order, and without established statutes, a Cyclops has no civilized way of life. He remains a hunter-gatherer, doing no work, gaining no rewards from the company of others, each living a brutish existence with his family that is apart from his fellows.

Similar themes – of beasts acting without productive effort, and without order or laws, in contrast to man – were also expressed by the poet Hesiod in his *Works and Days*:

> Take this to heart, Perses, and listen now to justice (*dikê*) For Zeus has ordained this law (*nomos*) to man, that fish and animals and birds should eat one another, for justice is not in them; but Zeus gave justice to man, and that is far best. For Zeus grants prosperity to whoever knows and speaks justice; but whoever lies and takes false oaths, and greatly harms justice, that man is left obscure forever. (Hesiod, *Works and Days* 275-84)

In this passage, Hesiod is asking his relative, Perses – perhaps his brother – not to press an unjust lawsuit against him for his inheritance. There is a law (*nomos*) for animals, but it is the way of tooth and claw, for beasts do not participate in justice and have no sense of right. Hesiod wants Perses to know that it is better for man to go by justice (*dikê*) than to attack other men. Hesiod is demonstrating his concern for the deliberated justice of *dikê*, which, from this time forward, will be a central concern of Greek thinkers and lawgivers.

But Hesiod is also comparing the use of violence by animals – who take what they want by force – to Perses' use of a false oath to obtain a crooked decision. Such fraud undercuts justice by subverting the ability to determine 'straight justice' in real cases. Fraud is a form of *hubris*, or 'outrage', an attack on the honour, possessions or status of another person. Hesiod's condemnation of *hubris* presumes that there is some sense of justice that even the magistrates and courts must not violate, and that to do so is an offence against the gods that usurps their rightful authority. In Hesiod's world, when justice is perverted, the result is the retribution of Zeus – the ultimate source of justice in the world. The customs of justice in the community allowed Hesiod's audience to understand that *hubris* was to be condemned, and that *dikê* was a better alternative.

Dikê is probably derived from the Greek verb *deiknumi*, to 'show' or to 'point'. Perhaps the first instance of *dikê* involved two farmers who were arguing over the boundary between their plots of land. *Iliad* 12.421-4 has two farmers fighting over such a boundary line, in a scene that is used to vivify the fighting between the Greeks and the Trojans. 'Straight *dikê*' (*orthê dikê*) would be the straight line between them, to which a mediator or arbitrator would point, and which would resolve their contention with a settlement that was fair to both sides. It is better, Hesiod maintains, for Perses and himself to resolve their dispute amicably, rather than to use false oaths that pervert the administration of justice for fraudulent ends.

I have translated *dikê* as 'justice', which is in one sense the process of bringing a resolution to a particular case, according to some standard of fairness. *Dikê* here may be contrasted with *themistes*, decrees by an authority that were imposed, often with divine sanction. But *dikê* has a deeper meaning than the decision of a judge: it is a sense of right and of balance that must underlie any such resolution, and that is the foundation of our human way of life. The way in which *dikê* is understood and used in different cities may vary – the justice of Sparta will not be the same as that in Athens – but the underlying notion that some standard of right is necessary for civilized life is always there. For the Cyclopes and other beasts, it is enough to lunge forth and act as each *can*. But man must properly act as he *should*. To do this in a political community he needs a *nomos*, or law, that is based on a proper sense of right.

Nomos means 'law', but this too has wide and narrow meanings. Widely, it means certain standards, or broad norms from which particular decisions may be derived; it is the customs on which a society is based, which may or may not be written. For Hesiod, the *nomos* is that men and animals act in different ways: the one by force and the whim of the moment, and the other by productive effort, deliberation and justice. In later times, however, *nomos* will take on a narrower meaning. The *nomoi* are general principles and rules, arrived at by an accepted process of deliberation, carved into stone in public view, enforced as laws, and immutable except by special act.

There is a lot more to *themis, dikê* and *nomos* than can be said here, and many complexities and qualifications to be grasped, but in broad terms *themis* is the overall order governing the community which is established by the gods and the decrees of rulers; *dikê* is the balance between disputing parties, as well as a way to resolve actual disputes, under an order proper to human beings; and *nomos* (or a *nomos*) is the law (or a law) that is instituted to accomplish this. It may be helpful to remember that Hesiod, in his *Theogony*, finds the mythological birth of

Fig. 5. Rhamnous, Attica. Site of the Temple of Nemesis and the Statue of Themis.
Photograph by the author.

Dikê – personified as a goddess – from *Themis*. *Dikê* is the sister of Peace
(*Eirênê*) and Good Order (*Eunomia*) (Hesiod, *Theogony* 901-2). *Themis*
is the wider idea, of which *Dikê, Eirênê* and *Eunomia* are narrower aspects
of order. *Nomos* is the law – and *nomoi* the laws – that people enact, in
order to live in a just, and orderly, way. The lawgiver – the establisher of
thesmoi and *nomoi* – will base his statutes and laws on a certain conception

of *dikê*, and he will ask his fellows to habituate themselves to following his laws.

Ethos and *nomos*

The customs and institutions of justice in Hesiod are more developed than in Homer, and magistrates are coming to assume the roles of arbitrators, in terms that are no longer voluntary for the parties. But their decisions are still highly customary, and based upon norms that were shared in the community, rather than hard and fast laws that were formally deliberated, enacted and enforced. Prior to written law, what kinds of customs, rules or laws did such judges follow? In many cases they had only their sense of fairness, habits based on the unwritten cultural norms of the day, the prerogatives they saw as due to those involved, as well as an ability to bring opponents into agreement. There is a sense of order in Homer's men, for instance, but it has not been defined in a set of laws. On a deep level it is not in *nomos,* but rather in *ethos*: the unwritten customs and habits that underlie human life and action.

In *Iliad* 1, Achilles and Agamemnon fall into conflict, and Achilles reaches for his sword. Each is pursuing his own honour, in the form of loot taken in battle, using the norms and actions that each has habituated. At that moment Athena appears to Achilles alone, urging him to stay his hand for the moment, to attack Agamemnon with words rather than violence, in order to get three times more in the future. Athena may represent a calm, deliberative state of mind, in a man who is able to consider the long-range implications of his actions, and overcome the habits of violence he has accepted. Such an *ethos* is a precondition to any acceptance of the laws, for every litigant must restrain the desire for vengeance and accept the verdict rendered. This is the birth of man the ethical being, able to consider right and wrong before acting. This does not mean, of course, that Achilles rejects the prevailing norms of the day, or that he accepts Agamemnon's decision; it does mean that the violence is forestalled for the moment, and Achilles takes out his anger in a different way.

At the start of the *Iliad*, Achilles' anger clouds his judgement, and prevents him from reconciling with Agamemnon and returning to the battle. In Book 9, when an embassy of Greeks tries to convince Achilles to return to the battle, Ajax points out to Achilles that even the brother of a man slain accepts a payment for the killing, and allows his desire for vengeance to be calmed. But Achilles has a heart that is beyond such pacification; for the sake of a single slave girl he is willing to jeopardize the entire mission, even though the embassy has brought seven young maidens to him (*Iliad* 9.632-6). At the end of the *Iliad*, when the Trojan king Priam comes to Achilles and asks for his son Hector's body back, Achilles tells Priam 'don't provoke me', lest he be unable to control himself (*Iliad* 24.560-1).

In each of these cases, a precondition to a peaceful solution is for each of the parties – especially Achilles – to stay his anger, place himself under proper self-control, and listen to proposed resolutions. The solution is not at all legal, but rather ethical; it relates to the *ethos* of a man such as Achilles. Will he follow the prevailing *ethos* of loot and violence, or can he hold his emotions under such control, and avoid violence?

Hesiod gives us his own views of this issue, in his *Works and Days* (lines 137ff.). In his mythological construction of the races of men who lived before his own, Hesiod saw an order (*themis*) for the earlier races that was based on an *ethos* (*kata ethea*). This order required proper sacrifices to the gods, as well as good relations with one's fellows, and included an existence free of strife, backbreaking work and suffering. It is a failure in the *ethos* – a failure to follow the implicit sense of right – that brought trouble to these earlier races. This failure is associated with foolishness (*aphradiês*), outrageous behaviour (*hubris*) and wickedness (*atasthalia*). Each race became progressively less fortunate than the previous, the result being the present race of iron, which needs a firm sense of law (*nomos*) and its administration.

An *ethos* is dependent upon the ideals that each person is exposed to, accepts and habitually practises. The nature of the *ethos* in a political community is of vital importance, for it shapes – and is shaped by – the way of life its people accept. The archaic poet Xenophanes, living in the sixth century BC, offered his view of a good *ethos* (poem 1). His poem on the *symposium* presents the scene of a drinking party that may serve as a microcosm of the *polis* and the need for a decent *ethos* in its citizens. Xenophanes sings of standing around the *kratêr* – the bowl in which water and wine were mixed – in a home with a clean floor and clean discourse, abundant food and sweet smells, proper respect for the gods, and good cheer (*euphrosunê*). To maintain this sense of conviviality and prevent the violence of aggrieved drinkers, harsh words must be avoided. Avoid the old stories, Xenophanes writes, those of battles with centaurs and of violent feuds, for they lead to no good. Speak rather cheerfully, with calmness and respect for the gods; maintain a calm state of mind, and a proper *ethos*, lest violence erupt.

Solon, singing some two centuries after Homer, also recognized the need to calm the spirit of anger that may threaten his *polis* with strife, but for Solon, the matter has become not only one of receiving just compensation, but of accepting the need for restraint before the laws in one's own actions. In his poem 36, he writes of slaves, trembling before the *êthê* – the habits of mind, the characters, or perhaps the whims – that lead their masters to violence and slavery (36.14). The answer to this, Solon writes in his poem 4, is Lawfulness, *Eunomia*, which

> smoothes what is rough; quells anger, dims *hubris*
> and shrivels the flowering bud of arrogant destruction.
>
> (Solon 4.34-5)

It is Solon's task to change the underlying ethical habits needed for proper acceptance of the laws, as much as it is to write the laws themselves. Such traditions often connect lawgivers to reforms in poetry and music, both of which can affect the *ethos* of the citizens. Two hundred years after Solon, in the fourth century BC, Plato would take the idea of controlling the poets to a strong conclusion, in his *Republic*, by claiming that the ideal city must be purged of poets who threaten its harmony by their unseemly verses. Aristotle, in his *Politics*, also saw a need for proper education in a good city. In every case, the Greeks knew that it was vital to foster the proper state of mind, good moral values and habits that lie at the base of all good relations in the *polis*. Respect for the laws requires the willingness to forego the personal satisfaction of vengeance. Whatever the sense of justice and the manner of administering it in any particular city, the values and habits of the Greeks determined what kind of laws they established, and how – or whether – they followed them.

Public law

In most of the scenes described above, an inability to resolve – or at least temper – a conflict can have catastrophic consequences for the community. In Homer's world, Agamemnon and Achilles are leaders of their own contingents of soldiers, and should Achilles kill Agamemnon, violent strife between the Greeks would surely decimate their ranks. In Hesiod, should Perses continue his fraud against Hesiod, the procedures of justice will be corrupted, and, as Hesiod puts it, the Justice of Zeus will fall on everyone. The symposium scene described by Xenophanes will be entirely disrupted, should one drunken attendee rise to violence. There are, in other words, implications for everyone, should injustice anywhere lead to violence. The recognition that some disputes are not matters of concern to the parties alone, but concern everyone, and must be deliberated in public forums, marks the first steps in the birth of public law.

In Book 18 of the *Iliad* (lines 490-540) Homer leaves us a picture of two cities, and two ways of life, the City of Peace and the City of War, inscribed on the great Shield of Achilles. In the City of War, there are ambushes, battles and killing. It is the other – the City of Peace – that is important to us here. In this city there were marriages and celebrations, young people dancing, lyres and flutes playing. Yet during the merriment a dispute about a murder has broken out in the centre of town over whether one man has paid the blood price for another he has slain. Homer presents the scene vividly, even if its meaning is difficult to grasp. The two men faced each other while their supporters were loudly gathering into groups on either side. The scene is not one of quiet contemplation; it is raucous almost to the point of violence. There is a need for positive restraints upon the townsmen; the heralds of the city were trying to keep the two sides separated. The elders had gathered in the middle of the circle, each trying to offer a solution that could dampen the conflict. On the ground was a sum of gold, to be given to the judge who offered a straight decision, or perhaps to the winning disputant. The scene is fraught with problems of interpretation, but the general picture is of a strife that is being controlled by some process of mediation.

The question at hand is not about the guilt of one party; he has killed a man, this is certain. The question is over how the desire for retribution is to be satisfied. The disputants are looking not for an absolute standard of justice or written laws, but rather to a decision that can satisfy both parties and end the strife. A 'just' decision is one that both sides can agree on, and that forestalls a violent clash. This is dispute mediation, not the application of justice as we think of it in courts today; the disputants are under pressure from the crowds to resolve their dispute, but they are not required to accept any particular resolution. It is important to note that the 'City of Peace' is not a town in which no disputes occur; it is the way that disputes are handled that distinguishes it from the City of War. Whichever one of the elders who proposes a solution that satisfies the family or friends of the dead man, and to which the killer can agree, will have benefited the community at large.

The leaders, mediators, arbitrators or judges calm the tensions, and bring a resolution before the violence can spread. The Greeks were coming to recognize that matters of law were not just matters between feuding opponents; some matters concerned the entire city, and judgements of those matters – and the ability to enforce the decision – had to be placed under public control. The entire community is on the verge of violence. The result of this is the growth of public law, or law in which the community takes a stake in the outcome, and exercises jurisdiction over the decision. In our own day, a matter such as murder is not up to the family or friends of the deceased to prosecute; it is up to a public prosecutor.

The most important advance here may be in the laws of Solon. His poem fragment, cited above, tells the Athenians that lawfulness – a state of mind conducive to following the laws, rather than acting with personal violence – is the key to ending destruction in the city. But what is the nature of such a threat, and where does it come from? The actions of unjust individuals – especially the leaders of the people – start with acts of *hubris*, arrogant actions, that destroy a sense of justice and lead to violence. As a result,

> with rapaciousness they rob from one another,
>   and fail to guard the sacred foundations of Justice
> who silently knows what is and what was.
>   But, in time, retribution certainly comes.
> And now this inescapable wound comes to the entire city,
>   which falls swiftly into an evil slavery.
> It awakens civil strife and sleeping tribal war … (4.13-19)

The key here is that the strife comes to the *entire polis*; no one can escape; even someone hiding in the bedroom of his own home – think of a rich aristocrat who tries to wait out the civil disorder by hiding in a walled compound – will suffer from this. The result was not only a moral injunction to accept the lawfulness that civilized life requires, but also a sense of laws as *public*. One of Solon's innovations was not only to write the laws publicly – others had done that – but also to make it possible for anyone to who wishes to do so (*ho boulomenos*) to initiate a lawsuit. Law was no longer to be a matter only for the parties involved, but anyone who thinks himself aggrieved can demand that his case be heard. This is the development of true public law, in which any free adult male can sue anyone other (recognizing that there can be serious consequences for bringing a frivolous suit) because preserving justice is important to everyone. It is vital, then, that the community have a solid set of laws to live by, and proper institutions for their interpretation and enforcement.

Substantive and procedural laws

The Greeks' concern for fairness, achieved through a just process of deliberation between the two parties, lends a particular flavour to Greek laws and their use, which is often foreign to our own way of thinking.

Consider these two laws, and the differences between them. The first is from the law code of Hammurabi, a non-Greek law based around an early Babylonian leader in the ancient Near East:

> If a builder has built a house for a man and his work is not strong, and if the house he has built falls and kills the householder, let the builder be killed. (*The Hammurabi Code*, no. 229)

This law – written in the form of a conditional, 'if-then' statement – offers a definition of the crime, and prescribes the penalty for running foul of it. Thus it is strongly substantive: it gives us the substance of the crime and the punishment. But it offers no procedures by which a decision should be reached; perhaps the king (Hammurabi) or one of his officials will make a decision, or perhaps the law simply allows the family of the victim to pursue revenge without threat of counter-attack. The ability to put forth, apply, and enforce the law all belong to a single authority. Perhaps this 'law' is how Hammurabi, as a judge, ruled in one particular case; he may be laying this down as a precedent for future cases, or rather proclaiming his own status as a shepherd to his people and the voice of the gods. In any event, there is nothing here to tell us *how* to determine the facts of the case, and *whether* this law (or another) applies. There are no checks specified against a judge – or a tyrant – who misapplies the law.

Now consider this Greek law from Gortyn:

> Whatever is written for the judge to decide, by witnesses or by an oath of denial, he shall decide as written. But in other matters he shall decide on oath according to the pleas. (XI.26)

There are written laws, and the judge must follow them – but the *content* of those laws is not given. We are rather told *how* the case should be resolved – by the use of written laws as they apply to witnesses and oaths, or according to pleas. The magistrate must make certain that the proper procedures have been followed: that the accused party was summoned, that witnesses were produced, that an oath was administered, etc. But the substance of the judgement – what a 'straight judgment' means – was left to the decision of the people involved, to be judged according to the laws. The final decision would have been highly dependent upon the content of the oath. An underlying sense of right in the parties – and in the judges – remained very important, especially for those many areas for which no laws had been written.

The distinction between *substantive* and *procedural* laws is vital. A 'substantive' law is a rule that dictates the content of a decision – as in Hammurabi's law. But such a substantive sense of law is little seen in the shield scene in Homer, and has little place in the Dreros, Chios and Gortyn examples; their focus is on what procedures should be followed. In Homer's City of Peace, the village elders, in the middle between the opponents, have no case law to refer to and no substantive rules; they have only their sense of fairness, and their customs and values, which include the need for payback to satisfy the aggrieved party. They play out their drama in a scene that is highly formulaic and ritualistic. There is no monarch and his rules, akin to Hammurabi and his laws, to dictate the decision. The Greek stress on following proper procedures – not on imposing rules – will be fundamental to our understanding of Greek laws throughout history.

Chapter 3

The Lawgiver and his Laws

Early judges

In the Shield of Achilles scene in Homer, the elder who brings a successful resolution to the dispute does an important service to the community, and gains a well-deserved reputation for his ability to calm the storms of anger that accompany disputes. Early judges likely rose to prominence because of their reputations for fairness, the support they could get from various factions, and their ability to end disputes and return the *polis* to a normal state of affairs. Such figures of justice appear often in history; perhaps the ancient Hebrew king Solomon is the best known. There is a picture of what appears to be such a man in the *Histories* of Herodotus (1.96-100). The story is unlikely to be factual, but it presents a plausible way by which a person's reputation as a mediator could spread, as well as Herodotus' view, in the fifth century BC, of how a tyrant might arise. One Deioces, a Mede (from Asia Minor), was a wise man, who gave judgements and resolved disputes across a wide area. By conscious design, he became a figure of justice, and his reputation spread. He was always available to hear disputes, and the people relied upon him to bring calm resolution to what could have become violent. He became very valuable, if not irreplaceable, to them.

Had Deioces established a more comprehensive set of norms or rules that others could have used, he would have become a lawgiver. Had he stabilised the political situation, and then stepped aside to let others participate, he could have at least become a legitimate official. But he did neither; justice remained personal to him, expressed in individual cases rather than a set of laws, and administered as he alone chose. Deioces actually wanted to become a tyrant, and after he had made himself indispensable, he withdrew from judging cases – an action that left a serious possibility of conflict in the area. He returned only when the people granted him absolute power, a personal bodyguard, and a huge fortress. He becomes the exact antithesis of the lawgiver – a despot seeking personal power, more akin to an eastern king than to a Greek man of justice.

The story of Deioces indicates the close connection between a reputation for justice and political power, and demonstrates the sometimes ambiguous nature of a political ruler who is also a man of justice. But such a man does not rise above his own personal decisions, and the order he establishes will likely not last beyond his own day. He rules by personal reputation and the support of others, but he establishes no long-range ethical norms or written laws that can last beyond his own lifetime. He becomes the antithesis of a lawgiver – a man who rules by personal whim rather than by laws. His way of doing business is appropriate for those willing to live under the authority of a particular man, but it is in no way proper for a *polis* of citizens, living under laws. What they need is a lawgiver, not a tyrant – someone to bring a rational order to their *polis*, and to provide laws by which they can govern themselves.

Civic crisis and the lawgiver's solution

Hesiod knew that man has the capacity for justice – but how this should be conceived, and implemented, in any particular *polis* is not self-evident. Aristotle, in Book 1 of his *Politics*, maintained that the *polis* develops naturally – it exists 'by nature' given our own natures as political animals – but that this does not mean that justice is automatic. The development of a Greek *polis* was often punctuated by periods of civil strife, in which lawful order broke down, factional conflicts engulfed the community, and gangs competed for control. At times a single tyrant may take control. It was in response to a civic crisis that the citizens may call upon a man, renowned for his wisdom and justice, and beholden to neither side in the conflicts, to mediate their disputes and bring order to the community.

The members of the community were making a strong statement about the kind of *polis* they wanted; they were willing to break with traditions and to reshape their *polis* as reason dictated. Greek cities became, as Oswyn Murray put it, 'Cities of Reason': organized and governed as their citizens determined was proper, rather than by the inherited habits of the past. The lawgiver was able to provide an alternative to the accepted order, which many might have thought was derived from the gods, but that had failed to bring them the order, peace and stability they needed.

Such a man, and his deeds, soon attained a legendary reputation. The scholar Andrew Szegedy-Maszak has described several principal stages common to the legends surrounding the various lawgivers. It would be wrong to ascribe this pattern of development to every Greek *polis*, and we must recognize that these stages are taken from legends, which change in the telling. Nevertheless, the legends show remarkable consistency, and given what we do know about the early lawgivers, the legends do not contradict what we otherwise know about the early *poleis*. This suggests an historical basis for the legends.

In the first, initial, stage, the *polis* falls into strife and conflict. Social pressures in the *polis*, whether between rich and poor, or competing factions, lead to a breakdown in civic order which threatens to erupt into warfare. There can be different ways to relieve the pressure, including the removal of a rival faction by authorizing a colony, in which some citizens form their own *polis* and live away from their former home. But to resolve the tensions permanently, the citizens ask a man of great reputation, acceptable to all parties, to stand between them as an impartial judge, to write (or rewrite) their laws, and to bring about a solution. This middle, or 'medial', stage suggests strong parallels to the Homeric City of Peace, in which two disputants ask for a solution from the elders. Similarly in the *polis,* the lawgiver steps up, addresses the disputes with a series of reforms, but also establishes a comprehensive set of written laws. This solidifies the community's rules and sets them above the power of any particular person to change.

His actions and his laws, however, do not placate everyone, and the lawgiver is buffeted by demands that he adapt his laws to their particular wishes. They might have pressured him to grant a judgement contrary to the laws, for reasons of friendship, wealth, family, etc. Although made objective through public display, the laws do not yet stand on their own as an independent standard of justice. The people are still focused on the lawgiver as a person to judge their disputes. To establish the laws, and not any particular man, as the final authority in the *polis*, the lawgiver has the people take an oath to follow the laws for a set period of time (ten years or more) or until he returns from a journey. In this final, third stage, the lawgiver goes into exile. Without him there to mitigate their individual cases, or to change the laws, and given their oaths to follow the laws, the people must turn to the laws as their highest authority, thus ingraining them into the fabric of civic life. In the process of these three stages, the *polis* itself passes from a state of lawlessness (*dusnomia*) to lawfulness (*eunomia*).

According to such traditions, an early lawgiver establishes a common form of justice, and a common code of rules, that are applicable to all, and that stand with an authority above any particular person or group of persons. The laws may be oral decrees, such as the laws of Lycurgus in Sparta, but are usually written laws, such as those of Solon in Athens. Whether or not the traditions accurately reflect what happened to the lawgiver in any real situation, it is the case that the laws must rise to a status above the capacity of any particular person to change. The law-giver's creation of a *nomos* that exists apart from anyone's particular *ethos* gives the *polis* a way to maintain its order, in a way that is not dependent upon the good graces of any particular person. The *polis* passes from rule by men, to rule under laws.

The advent of written laws

The centrepiece of the lawgiver's work is his law code. Sparta is the most important example of a *polis* that ran on purely oral laws; it is said that its ancient lawgiver, Lycurgus, had a law forbidding the writing of his laws. In such a state, the laws are more maxims than legal rules, they function by the shared ideals of the people involved, and rely upon the preservation of the maxims in oral injunctions passed on and enforced. But Sparta was in many ways unique. Such a law 'code' is surely more of an *ethos* than a true code of laws. To become an objective part of civic life, the laws must be written and placed into public view.

The precise dating of the first Greek written laws is not possible; but by the seventh century BC the practice was spreading. It is interesting that the earliest written laws in Greece were not from the Greek mainland, but rather from colonies, especially in the west (Sicily and southern Italy). These colonies were less bound to maintain the deep traditions of their mother cities; they were starting new lives, and were able to shape their laws as their new conditions required. Even though we have the most information about laws – especially written laws – from Athens and from Crete, we should recognize that some of the lawgivers we see as minor today may have been highly innovative, even though their cities did not rise to the cultural heights or historical renown of Athens.

The new laws may have held various relationships to the existing customs and laws of the community. Some laws may have codified and frozen traditional norms and rules, such as Draco's laws in Athens. His solution was not to innovate, but rather to prevent the kind of innovation that can lead to instability in the community or a sense of outrage among those who think that their traditional prerogatives are being violated. Other lawgivers may have offered a truly new vision of life, as part of more radical social changes; Solon, who followed a generation after Draco, is a good example. Others may have put the norms of the aristocracy into written form, thus preserving their authority albeit accepting the need to place these norms into public view, and allowing public deliberation.

The impetus for such changes may have come from different direc-tions, with different purposes held by different parties leading to different results. In some cases, people outside the aristocracy may have felt that the aristocrats were abusing their prerogatives, and acting arbitrarily in the administration of justice, a position exemplified by the peasant poet Hesiod. In a parallel, the so-called Twelve Tables of Roman Law, enacted in Rome in the mid-fifth century BC, are often seen as a response to the so-called 'struggle of the orders,' a political struggle between the traditional aristocracy in Rome and the people without aristocratic birth. Such reforms may also come from concessions by the aristocracy to prevent unrest, as part of a reaction by the aristocracy to challenges to their prerogatives. The Greek poets Theognis and Alcaeus represent the aristocracy; they express outrage at the declining power of the traditional nobility, in the face of a so-called *nouveau riche* class of people who were gaining money without aristocratic birth. Lycurgus, the lawgiver of Sparta, rather cemented a place for a citizen-warrior class, which would impose its rules by force over others.

The written laws become norms which limit the magistrates' range of acceptable actions. (The lawgiver's traditional exile removes his own ability to change the laws.) This limits their options, and restrains them from making decisions that might be customarily correct, but that do not agree with the laws. It is likely, for instance, that debt slavery had arisen in Athens near the end of the seventh century BC, perhaps as an assertion of prerogatives by an aristocracy (either of birth or wealth) against poor farmers. Solon's injunctions against such slavery – expressed in his poem 36, preserved in *Constitution of the Athenians*, section 12 – would have precluded magistrates from allowing such slavery.

Written laws serve to stabilize life in the *polis*. The Greeks, tradition tells us, could make it very difficult to change a law. One story had it that the city of Locris on southern Italy had a law requiring anyone who wanted to change a law to argue for the change while standing with his head in a noose (Demosthenes 24.139; Polybius 12.16); in addition to Zaleucus of Locris, Charondas of Catana was also credited with this law (Diodorus 12.17). In the late fifth century, the orator Antiphon said that the long age of a law is proof of its excellence (5.14; 6.2). In the last decade of the Peloponnesian War, the Athenians realized that the democratic assembly had been acting rashly and outside the law, so they established officials to reinscribe the laws of Solon, in order to restrict the assembly from passing decrees that contradicted the written laws.

We often speak of 'law codes' in ancient Greece and elsewhere. But this is actually a misnomer. A 'code' of laws implies a system of organization, arranged by subject or other criteria, and purporting to be comprehensive. Ancient laws, whether of the Greeks or earlier, in the ancient

Near East, are more properly 'lists'. Even in the most developed of the classical Greek cities, such as Athens, and in the most comprehensive of the inscribed laws we have, those of Gortyn, the laws are more ad hoc than systematic. This is an outgrowth of several issues in Greek life. The first is the very openness – the open texture, to cite the modern legal theorist H.L.A. Hart – of the courts for the Greeks. The greatest ancient concern was that each party have equal time to speak his case (the classical Athenians used a water-clock to keep the times equal). But what each party could say was wide open; there were no rules of evidence. Further, since the laws were generally written in response to particular issues of concern, there was no attempt to be systematic, and no compilations of modern or even Roman kinds.

Roman law was far more systematic – and comprehensive – than the laws of the Greeks. The Romans faced different problems than did the Greeks. The Greeks needed to bring order without tyranny to their particular *poleis* – each of which remained independent and self-governing, with its own customs, religious rituals and institutions. The citizens of any particular *polis* could rely upon the unspoken, assumed norms that they shared, and never needed to bring consistency to the laws of different *poleis*. The Romans, however, ruled hundreds of cities from Rome. They had to find a way to determine what was common to all people everywhere (the 'law of peoples', *ius gentium*), while making allowances for the local differences (the 'civil law', *ius civile*). To judge a dispute between a Roman and a Sicilian, they had to account for the different customs in the two areas, while finding common ground between them. This required a much more systematic understanding and codification than the Greeks ever needed. The political form of the *polis* set basic limits to the understanding of the laws that the Greeks could develop.

Just how hard it may be for those not deeply immersed in the customs and affairs of a particular *polis* to interpret its laws may be seen in this sixth-century BC law from Gortyn, on Crete:

> Gods. The *polis* gave the lands for planting in Keskoria and Palai to be planted. If anyone has bought or received any of them as a mortgage, [then] the transaction shall not be valid. It shall be impossible to take the mortgage in pledge before the usufruct is measured. (Arnaoutoglou no. 54)

To interpret and apply this law – really a rule applying to a particular geographic area and a particular type of agreement – we would have to answer a series of questions. Who were the lands given to, and why? What does 'bought or received' them mean – is it a 'property' transfer, a right to use them, a dowry, or a gift? Were there outstanding mortgages against those areas, and to whom, and in what terms? Does the English term 'mortgage' properly convey the status of such agreements at this time? Does 'usufruct' – a Latin legal term relating to the right to use a piece of property belonging to another without waste or destruction of its substance – adequately convey the agreement made and invalidated here? Why would 'the *polis*' invalidate that agreement in favour of planting by another? Was there an underlying motivation for this action by the *polis*? Was there a social crisis leading to such an action, or was it directed at some particular persons? Who is 'the *polis*' anyway? Which institution – or person(s) – made such a pointed decision with respect to these particular areas? What constitutional implications follow from this?

This law also illustrates an important linguistic formulation that we have already seen: *conditional statements*. A 'conditional' statement has two parts: the *protasis*, or an 'if' clause, that establishes the condition which, if fulfilled, makes the law applicable. The *apodosis* is the 'then' statement that must follow if the *protasis* is true. Such statements may be seen in the law of Dreros, the law of Solon in Demosthenes, and the law of Hammurabi, cited above.

The conditional statement is in the second sentence: If anyone has made a 'mortgage' agreement for these areas, then the agreement shall be invalidated. This would invalidate loans made against this land, by invalidating any contract or lawsuit taken with those lands as security. The law itself does not, however, say that 'no mortgages shall be valid' against these areas; it rather establishes the hypothetical condition first to delimit the application of the law (the law applies only IF such an agreement has been made), and then specifies the outcome (such an agreement shall be invalid). Laws, in other words, are projections into the future – they tell us what will happen, should some hypothetical event occur. The lawgiver is thus a wise man, who knows how to manage life in the *polis* beyond the present moment.

The conditional nature of such laws also allowed for an important advancement in the future: the capacity to deliberate both about the underlying facts of the case (is the 'if' clause true?) and the application of the law to it (does this particular law apply to this particular case, and how?). In later times these two aspects – matters of fact, and matters of law – would become distinct stages in the process of judging a case. The lawgiver provides the laws by which the case can be understood, once the facts are brought out by the parties and the witnesses.

Lawgivers and constitution-makers

Given the deep connection between *ethos* and *nomos*, and the many subtle customs and norms that are not spelled out in the laws, Aristotle considered it important to distinguish lawgivers from constitution-makers. The Greek political constitution is the *politeia*, the 'polis-ness' of the *polis*, the political and social organization as well as institutions and offices that give the *polis* its particular form. A lawgiver provides a set of laws that solves a social crisis without attempting to change the basic organization of the *polis*, while a constitution-maker goes more deeply into the moral and social norms by which the institutions and offices are organized.

Aristotle, in his *Politics*, distinguishes lawgivers (a *nomothetês* is a 'law-establisher') from constitution-makers (those who establish a *politeia* as well as writing laws). Those constitution-makers, Aristotle writes,

> after gaining personal experience by participating in *polis* affairs, became lawgivers either in their own cities or in certain foreign cities. Some of these merely drafted laws, but others, like Lycurgus and Solon, also established constitutions (*politeiai*); for they put in place both constitutions and laws (*nomoi*). (Aristotle, *Politics* 2.12)

To bring order to an archaic *polis* the constitution-maker has to change the basic form into which the *polis* has been constructed, including its social order but also the moral outlook of the people, leading them to the practice of certain virtues, including a sense of justice. He organizes institutions, a festival calendar, religious rituals, tribal divisions, and other means by which to arrange their activities. No area of *polis* life is off-limits to his reforms; he changes not only the laws of the *polis*, but the people's basic outlook upon the laws and the *polis*.

To the lofty status of constitution-maker, Aristotle elevates Solon and Lycurgus; others he describes as lawgivers only, for they write laws that do not reform the basic moral outlook of the *polis*, but put those norms into written form without fundamental changes. For instance, a constitution-maker determines the nature and organization of the political offices in the *polis*, while a lawgiver leaves those offices as they are, even as he writes laws to be followed by the officials.

The reputation of a constitution-maker was based not only on his laws, but on his fundamental effects upon the citizen-*ethos* of the *polis*. Such a constitutional lawgiver does more than tell the people to be excellent by following the laws; he tells them what excellence *is*. He not only enforces the requirements of *dikê;* he describes it, and gives them a vision of justice to follow in their lives. Solon's poem 4 is a powerful example of how he connects *dikê* to a sense of Good Order (*Eunomia*); in contrast, the poetry of Tyrtaeus laid down a sense of excellence for the Spartans that was anchored in fighting for Sparta. As a city planner today, or a zoning board, may presume to dictate the basic physical shape of a city, so the Greek constitution-maker shapes the moral and social order of the *polis*, carving its laws into stone, and engraving its moral precepts into the memories of its citizens.

Chapter 4

Minos and Rhadamanthus of Crete

The 'Cretanizing' Classical Greeks

The mythology and the history of Crete are closely intertwined – and not consistent. According to Homer's *Odyssey* (19.172-9), Crete was a land of 90 cities, thickly inhabited, fair and fruitful, with many tongues all mixed up. His depiction of Achaeans, Eteocretans, Cydonians, Pelasgians and three tribes of Dorians matches the evidence we have for its fragmented political nature, which lasted into the Hellenistic period and beyond. The early Linear 'A' tablets, superseded by Linear 'B' from the mainland, and followed by the non-Greek Eteocretan tongue in the archaic period, all attest to this political disunity.

Homer does say that Crete was ruled from the city of Knossos by King Minos, but we do not know what 'being ruled' means, how this 'rule' was maintained, or how long it lasted. Given the many political dynasties in later Greek history that lasted for two generations, it is possible that Minos' rule did not long outlast his own life. Herodotus (7.170-1) and Diodorus (4.79) claimed that Minos died on Sicily; that Crete was then depopulated by a failed military expedition, and that the local population was replaced three generations before the Trojan War. None of this suggests long-term constitutional unity and stability. Indeed it would be odd if Crete had been unified in the pre-archaic and archaic period.

But many of the later classical Greeks saw Crete quite differently: as a single political entity, with a single ancient constitution and laws that were worthy of great veneration (for example, in Aristotle, *Politics* 2.10). Our own modern term 'syncretism', meaning 'a uniting and blending together of different systems', derives from *sunkretizein*, 'to unite against a common enemy, in the manner of the Cretan cities', from *syn*-, 'with, together' plus *Kret*-, 'Cretan'. The 'Cretan constitution' became an exemplar for later Greeks, who claimed that other lawgivers had travelled to Crete for inspiration. Lycurgus of Sparta and Zaleucas of Locris were each said to have gone to Crete, and to have received wisdom passed down through Cretan and Locrian lawgivers (Aristotle, *Politics* 2.12). Athenians of the late seventh-century BC – perhaps Solon – were said to have called upon a Cretan to cleanse Athens and to re-establish its proper religious rituals (*Constitution of the Athenians* 1). Plato partakes of this tradition by setting his characters in the *Laws* on Crete, where they journey towards the birthplace of Zeus, the source of their laws.

Such political and legal unification is not historically accurate – at least not after the rule of Minos – but it served the principal purpose of a lawgiver tradition, which was to provide an anchor and a source of legitimacy for later laws. The 'Cretanizing' of the later Greeks – their attempts to mimic the culture and customs of Crete – is certainly understandable, given the highly advanced archaeological ruins still extant at the city of Knossos. But it makes it all the more difficult for us to separate the conceptions of the later Greeks, and the centuries of stories surrounding the early Cretans, from the historical facts.

Minos and Rhadamanthus

That Knossos thrived prior to the Trojan War (before *c.* 1200 BC) is confirmed by archaeology; but its political and social organization cannot be reconstructed. According to legend, Minos was the ancient King of the Minoans, the civilization centred on the city of Knossos. He was credited with divine origins by later Greeks. Zeus had carried Europa off from Phoenicia to Crete, and the result was Minos, and his brothers Rhadamanthus and another. This legend, as well as the claim that Minos built a navy while Rhadamanthus gave the Cretans their laws, suggests that there were interactions between Near Eastern peoples and the Cretans. This is not out of line with general disruptions that occurred in the Near East in the thirteenth century BC, the controversial 'invasions' of the so-called 'Sea Peoples'. Theseus of Athens – and his fabled killing of the Minotaur on Crete – may also have grown out of earlier stories, to become an explanation for the ancient origin of the Athenian constitution and laws.

Minos may also represent a dynastic title, a family of rulers, who unified the religious rituals and held central power over the island (Diodorus 4.60.2-5). Diodorus claims that there were two Kings named Minos, the first being the brother of the lawgiver Rhadamanthus, and the second being his grandson, the creator of the Cretan navy and the ruler of the surrounding Aegean. Plutarch, in his *Life of Theseus*, writes that people of the island Naxos speak of two men named Minos. This connects the story of Minos' rule – and the killing of the Minotaur – to Naxos, and perhaps to other islands in the Aegean Sea. In any event, 'Minos' may be an attempt by later Greeks to see the disparate laws of particular rulers as subsumed under a single figure. This began early in the oral traditions;

Homer in his *Odyssey* (11.568-71) has Minos in Hades, judging cases arising among the dead. It is noteworthy that the cases judged here are disputes *among* the dead, judged according to a standard of fairness, as if they were disputes on earth. (The idea that the souls of the dead themselves may be judged in the afterworld is a later idea, appearing first in Plato's *Gorgias*, 523e-24a.)

Cretan social practices may have been concerned with cults and festivals associated with Zeus Cretagenes, 'Zeus Cretan-born', who was worshipped in Gortyn, Lyttus and Lato. Zeus is mentioned on a Linear 'B' tablet found at Knossos, and may have fused with native Minoan goddesses. It is possible that the monarchy under Minos or his successors fragmented politically, and that many people set off as colonists, while the rest fell prey to visitors from the mainland. Similarly the story of Theseus and the Minotaur, in which Athenian youth were forced to go periodically to Crete, to be lost in the labyrinth and eaten by the Minotaur, may represent hostages taken by the Cretans in a conflict with Athens. Plutarch saw the labyrinth as merely a prison, and the Athenian youth as simply slaves, and the stories as connected to offerings made to Delphi. Whatever the actual sequence of events, Minoan power collapsed after the death of Minos, and stories of his fame and the laws attributed to Rhadamanthus were all that was left.

Minos and Rhadamanthus have limited historical value as lawgivers; neither is mentioned in any of the inscribed laws found on Crete, only in the later literary works. But they serve as legendary points of focus for the venerated laws of the Cretans, and in that sense serve to illustrate the power of the legends associated with such figures. Whether they actually existed becomes less important than the way that later Greeks used them to understand their own laws, by anchoring them to an ancient, venerable past.

Thaletas

Thaletas, perhaps of Gortyn, Elyrus or Knossos, was a lyric poet alleged to have lived in archaic Crete during the seventh century BC. (He must not be confused with Thales, the philosopher of Miletus.) He is said to have brought certain norms of justice to Crete through his poetry and his music, perhaps using choral lyric poetry with dance to promote aristocratic norms. The inscription from Dreros suggests that officials held great personal responsibility under the laws; Thaletas may be a name associated with such personal efficacy. The Gortyn Code indicates a secretary or perhaps a recorder (xi.14-17) involved in the writing of the laws. The figure of the *dikastês* – the special judge or juror – may have begun to emerge. Thaletas may again suggest an embodiment of these trends in a single person, a judge, lawgiver and poet with a reputation for great wisdom.

Thaletas also epitomizes Sparta's use of Crete as an example for its customs and laws. Plutarch claims that when Lycurgus left Sparta, in order to avoid a conflict over the throne, he travelled to Crete among other places (Plutarch, *Lycurgus* 4). There he befriended Theletas, and convinced him to bring his songs – which promulgated obedience and harmony – to Sparta. Legends suggest that an oracle from Delphi legitimated this visit, thus casting a divine umbrella over Thaletas' words. He may have cured a plague or ended a civil war in Sparta with his songs and dances, which were used in public rituals to unite the Spartans in common activities. In this way he is said to have prepared the ground for Lycurgus, embedding the norms and rituals necessary for a more specific educational and political programme in his poetry. He thus also represents a merger of the poet, the educator and the political actor; he is said to have founded a training institution at Sparta, and to have used his poems to bring about a political result for Sparta. It is fascinating that the Spartans looked to Crete for an early source of the foundations needed for their laws, and found them in a poet / dancer.

Epimenides

Early laws and lawgivers were closely connected to religious rituals, for it is through such rituals that social and political order was maintained. Another seventh-century Cretan figure, whose historical reality cannot be separated from the mythology associated with him, is Epimenides. The Aristotelian *Constitution of the Athenians* has him summoned to Athens in the late seventh century, to purify the city from a religious crime associated with the attempted coup attempt of Cylon, and which put the Alcmaeonid family under a curse lasting centuries. By this story, Solon may have called Epimenides in, to purify the city of its blood pollution and re-establish proper religious rituals in Athens. This would put him in Athens some time closely after 621 BC or so. The relationship between Epimenides and the lawgiver Solon again suggest the close connections between the laws and religious rituals, as well as between Athens and Crete.

In the *Laws*, Plato's character Clinias the Cretan has Epimenides receiving an oracle to go to Athens ten years before the Persian attack, in 500 BC (*Laws* 642D). Such conflations of time, impossible to reconcile with other sources, are common for such a figure, and indicate the mutability of the legends. Little more historical evidence can be recovered about Epimenides; again, his import is in the way he was used, by later writers, to connect deep issues of customs, religious rituals, and laws to the early Cretans. Athenians and Spartans both claimed that their lawgivers benefited from early Cretan influences.

Later written laws on Crete

The many inscriptions of laws on Crete generally reflect attempts to formalize and preserve their earlier customs. The fragments of inscriptions from Eltyna, Lyttus, Eleutherna, Axus, Prinias and Dreros – and the more comprehensive stones of Gortyn – are not the work of ivory-tower theorists creating systematic, comprehensive codes, but rather the reduction to writing of the norms and procedures accepted in the towns in which they were written. None of these inscriptions connect early Crete to a lawgiver, but each rather suggests a process of writing that extended over time. It was the mainland Greeks, with their propensity for traditions anchored in a venerable origin, who used Crete as an anchor for their own laws, by trying to connect their early past with that of Crete. The legends of the early lawgivers of Crete say more about the views of the later mainland Greeks than about the early Cretans.

Chapter 5

Lycurgus of Sparta

Tyrtaeus and early Sparta

The Spartans embodied their entire way of life in the figure of their semi-legendary lawgiver, Lycurgus. His importance begins with the nature of the Spartan order that was attributed to him, and his connection to each Spartan's identity as a warrior and a member of an elite group of citizens. But this citizen *ethos* grew out of Sparta's early history, in which the Spartans engaged in a series of wars, over centuries, to subdue the area of Messene to their west. These were the three so-called Messenian Wars, which began in the eighth century BC and stretched into the sixth. The Spartans' obsession with maintaining their way of life became an obsession to maintain their dominance over the people they controlled – and to praise the virtues this required.

The Spartans first identified these wars, and the *ethos* that drove them to such successes, with the early poet Tyrtaeus, probably of the seventh century BC. He was possibly an Athenian, but this is also uncertain. If the stories are accurate, he rallied the Spartans to battle by inculcating a certain idea of *aretê*, or excellence, that was firmly rooted in military valour and service to Sparta. The Spartans would sing poems such as these before battle, and would transmit them to their children in order to preserve and extend the sense of community that was fundamental to Spartan life:

> To die falling in the front lines is a noble thing
>   for a brave man, fighting for his fatherland,
> Whereas leaving one's *polis* and rich fields
>   to live as a beggar is most painful of all things,
> Wandering with one's dear mother and aged father,
>   and one's small children and wedded wife.
> For he will be met with hostility by all those he comes upon,
>   having given over to need and hateful poverty.
> He disgraces his family, denies his splendid form,
>   and dishonor and evil accompany him.
>   …

Come on, young men, fight, standing by each other,
   don't run off shamefully or give way to fear,
but make your heart strong and courageous,
   and do not love your life when you are fighting men.
                                        (Tyrtaeus 10.1-10, 15-18)

A young man, fired up by such words, and seeking honour through solidarity with his fellows, would cringe at the thought of being outcast from the community due to cowardice. This has historical support from later times; after the battle of Thermopylae, in 480 BC, 300 Spartans chose to die rather than retreat before the Persians. Herodotus, in his account of the battle, tells us of a Spartan who survived, but was shunned when he returned home, and atoned for surviving by dying at a later battle. Another hung himself rather than live as a coward.

Such poetry, and the *ethos* it engenders, were wrapped up in a certain sense of excellence, or *aretê*, that was identified with courage, to stand fast with one's fellows in bloody slaughter, and to bend one's whole being towards the military defence of Sparta. In another poem, Tyrtaeus says that he would not take account of a man for athletic ability, great strength, handsomeness, material wealth, kingly status or eloquence. All that matters is a reputation for furious valour (*thouridos alkês*):

For a man is not good unless he can endure in war
   seeing the bloody slaughter,
   and can lunge at the enemy, standing close.
This is excellence (*aretê*), this is the best human prize
   and the fairest for a young man to carry.

For a young man who dies in battle, the entire community honours his name, he receives a fine memorial tomb, and his memory is kept alive for later generations. Given a passion for such excellence, the Spartan would be willing to endure much, with bloody ferociousness. Later Greeks, such as Aristotle, would recognize that the Spartans were very powerful when they needed one virtue – courage – but were at a loss when other virtues were needed. In any event, the Spartan *nomos* was not a written set of laws, but the norms of excellence associated with such poetry, and the social practices associated with them. The poetry, once memorized as a guide to conduct, became the *nomos* that guides the Spartans to excellence in service to Sparta. The actual organization of the citizen body remains impossible to verify, but would have included common meals, disciplined military units, and religious rituals.

Lycurgus and the Spartan order

Lycurgus is in many ways the model lawgiver, having created an overriding *ethos* and a set of oral ideals, rules and rituals designed to define and maintain the Spartan citizen order. The Spartans maintained this order for centuries. His laws were based on moral norms inculcated through a system of rigorous training and a hierarchical social order. According to tradition, he followed the path taken by many lawgivers, having travelled to Crete, Asia Minor, perhaps Egypt and to Delphi in the course of bringing his laws to Sparta. To cite one tradition, Lyttus, a Spartan colony on Crete, received many pre-Dorian traditions, perhaps established by King Minos of Crete, and then passed them on to Lycurgus during his visit (Herodotus 1.65; Aristotle, *Politics* 2.10). Lycurgus, having brought order to Sparta with his *nomos*, then left Sparta, so that the Spartans could follow his laws without his presence.

One must question Lycurgus' actual historical role in the development of this system; many aspects of it were probably grafted onto legends associated with him, thus turning him into a point of focus, and a legitimization, of the Spartan order that had developed over generations. Certain claims made for him – such as his establishment of the Spartan *gerousia*, or council of elders – are historically dubious at best. He embodies the characteristics of a lawgiver as a figure in a tradition, while his actual life is shadowy, semi-mythical, beyond the capacity to date with certainty, and truly timeless. Herodotus, Plato, Aristotle and Plutarch all attest to his importance, but Plutarch sums up the convolutions of stories around him by beginning his *Life of Lycurgus* with 'there is nothing indisputable to be said' about him.

The entire Spartan way of life was defined within a civic order designed to elevate the virtues of Tyrtaeus, to create the warriors able to practise them, and to give every person a place within that order. Lycurgus is credited with designing the laws needed to maintain that order, through an harmonious life at home, a sense of identity as a member of an elite, a sense of continuity passed on to their children, and a drive for dominance over their neighbours. A small group of citizens, the so-called *homoioi*, often translated as 'equals' but more accurately 'peers', constituted the citizen body in Sparta, each participating in civic life according to his place, and each dedicated to full-time service to the Spartan state. The later historian Polybius, in the second century BC, wrote that with respect to civic harmony, Lycurgus' wisdom was more divine than human (6.48).

The Spartan *homoioi* subjugated their neighbours in a way that was unseemly to other Greeks. The *perioikoi* were the 'dwellers around', those living in the immediate outskirts of Sparta, who had some rights but were not citizens. The *helots* were those living in the countryside, who had been reduced to a life of servitude, and who were forced to provide the food needed by the Spartan citizens. These were not chattel slaves – they were not owned by particular Spartans – but were made subservient to every Spartan, as if owned in common by all. To keep them in subjection, the Spartans used the virtues inculcated by Tyrtaeus. The Spartans declared war against them annually, thus claiming divine legitimacy for their unrelenting attacks, and they had a secret police force (the *krupteia*) to move among them and prevent anyone of prominence from rising in their midst. There is a story of 2,000 *helots* who came forth to assist Sparta, were honoured by the Spartans for their bravery, and then disappeared – killed for the threat contained in their bravery.

In political terms, Sparta is noteworthy for its reputation for never having lived under a tyranny, but rather under a particular form of *eunomia*, an orderly system of institutions, rituals and lawful conduct that regulated a person's activities from cradle to grave. Many aspects of this order were borrowed from elsewhere; Aristotle in *Politics* 2 claims that Crete was the source of much in the Spartan 'good order' (*eunomia*), including common meals and many of the offices. But the Spartan order was all-encompassing – and very stable – given its integration of individual activities, cult rituals, education, military training and political action into a coherent, albeit oppressive, social whole.

The political aspects of this order included two kings, passed down from ancient noble families; a Senate or 'gerousia' (council of elders); the assemblies of citizens, who might affirm or reject what is brought to them; and the ephors, or officials. This was supported by an economic order of equal land allotments between citizens, supported by the enslaved *helots*. The Spartan *eunomia*, or order, was rigid, stratified, and in many ways outright brutal – an expression of the underlying *ethos* that guided the Spartans.

The *Great Rhêtra*

The laws that Lycurgus brought to Sparta became known as the *Great Rhêtra*, or the great oral commandment. Spartan laws were not written – Lycurgus is said to have made a law in which it was expressly forbidden to reduce laws to writing – and in this sense we may ask whether he really brought laws to Sparta, or rather an *ethos* connected to social norms, institutions and rituals. The term *rhêtra* is connected to the Greek terms associated with rhetoric – such as *rhêtôr* 'public speaker', *rhêtoreia* 'oratory', and *rhêtos* 'expressly stated' – and means simply 'saying' or 'spoken agreement or commandment'.

According to Plutarch – himself a priest of Delphi – Lycurgus brought the *Great Rhêtra* back from Delphi after his father had been killed during a period of disorder. King Eurypon, who connected Lycurgus to the Eurypontid line of Spartan kings, had relaxed his rule in an attempt to garner popularity. But the people did not need a relaxed hand, and in the lawlessness that followed, Lycurgus' father was killed with a meat cleaver when trying to prevent a fight. He thus lost his life trying to stand in the middle of a dispute, a position generally associated with men of justice. Without an understanding of the need to obey laws, and without laws which the people should obey, attempts to loosen despotic rule were bound to end in conflict.

After his father's death, Lycurgus became the royal guardian of Sparta, until his brother's wife was with child. Lycurgus then gave up the crown and travelled: first to Crete, where he adopted laws from Thaletas, then to Asia Minor, where he encountered the works of Homer, and back to Sparta. Plutarch wrote that the Egyptians also claimed that he visited them, and brought back to Sparta their strict separation of a warrior caste from craftsmen and artisans. Enlightened by his experiences in the world, and desiring to bring a stable order to his *polis*, he returned to Sparta, and set about remaking the *polis* in the image of his ideas.

The *Great Rhêtra* itself, according to Tyrtaeus and preserved by Plutarch, came from the oracle at Delphi, and it commands the Spartans to:

> establish a sanctuary to Zeus Scyllanius and to Athena Scyllania, form tribes and obes [literally, to 'tribe' the people into tribes, and to 'obe' them into obes], establish a *gerousia* of thirty elders, including the leaders, and regularly call the people between Babyca and Cnacion [a bridge and a river?], make proposals and votes. The people shall make the final decision. (Tyrtaeus 4)

Lycurgus made deep changes to the social divisions and political offices in Sparta, established the Council of Elders or *gerousia*, and overcame the objections of the leading men to bring order to the *polis*. The oracle established a divine basis for the laws, and elevated Lycurgus over the petty demands of the individual Spartans. This may or may not be consistent with the historical reality – Plutarch says that Lycurgus appointed his friends into the first *gerousia* – but such institutions did achieve a long-term status, and the laws attributed to him did outlast particular men.

The oracle of Apollo can be found in the poems of Tyrtaeus:

> Having heard Phoebus (Apollo) they brought home from Pytho
>   (Delphi)
>   the oracles of the god and his predictions.
> Deliberations are to begin with the divinely honoured kings,
>   to whom the care of the lovely *polis* of Sparta is entrusted,
> and with the venerably-born elders; then the men of the people,
>   responding with straight *rhêtrais* (utterances),
> Are to speak fair words and do just deeds,
>   and not to counsel [crookedly] to the *polis*.
> The masses of the people will be followed by victory and power.
> For so was Apollo's revelation to the *polis*. (Tyrtaeus 4)

According to the customary laws of Sparta, the kings and elders were to begin deliberations about all proposals, which were then to be communicated to the masses of the people by their leaders. The people then affirm or veto the proposals given to them – they do not initiate their own proposals. It is likely that all of this had a deep resonance with the existing ways of doing things in Sparta, including the prerogatives of the existing noble families, and a need to prevent usurpations by the people. Such procedures were doubtless modified over years. For instance, Plutarch says that the ephors – the officials or civil magistrates in Sparta and other *poleis* who are not in the *Great Rhêtra* – were established 130 years after Lycurgus.

Later writers, such as Plato, Polybius and Plutarch, described Sparta's constitution as a 'mixed *politeia*', a mixture of various elements. For instance, the *gerousia* was intended to be a tempering element against the two kings, the monarchical element that otherwise might act rashly or against the needs of Sparta. Prior to this constitution, Plutarch also says, the *polis* was prone to move either towards tyranny (with too much power in the kings), or towards democracy (the unrestrained rule of the mob). The stability is interpreted by Polybius, who uses Sparta as an example for his own day, as reaching an even higher level in Rome. The Roman Republic did bear strong resemblances to the Spartan system, with its two consuls or high officials, its council of elders or Senate, and its various other officials and assemblies. But the Roman and Spartan systems developed, from the start, without awareness of such political concepts, by a historical process that is hidden to us. For the Spartans, this process has been embodied in the figure of Lycurgus, and connected by legends to early Crete, Asia Minor and Egypt.

If the social order associated with this political arrangement is extended out into the countryside, into the *perioikoi* and the *helots*, then Sparta may be seen as a social hierarchy, from noble kings and elders to abject serfs, each with a place in the order. The order brought by Lycurgus, which came after the subjugation of the countryside, then became a means to preserve the Spartan way of life. This encompasses a range of activities far beyond what we would consider to be part of a code of laws. Lycurgus is also credited with religious reforms, and within uniting Spartan life in the celebration of festivals, music and dance. The *Great Rhêtra* encompasses this order, and stands for an agreement by the people to follow the laws of Lycurgus, which were granted a divine sanction and a deep ancestry.

The Spartan system of training

Something more than social and political reforms was needed to keep such a system running, for any loss of a sense of order within Sparta could lead to drastic consequences. It would threaten the system of sustenance that allowed the Spartan *homoioi* to devote their full energies to military training, and could lead to devastating revolts in the countryside. The energy to maintain the order and prevent revolts was inculcated in the Spartan system of training, the *agôgê*, which was credited to Lycurgus. This life-long programme of training habituated every Spartan to the physical toughness needed to create the most feared land warriors in Greece. Plutarch observed that they were the only people in the world whose training was more arduous than actual warfare. (Plutarch, *Lycurgus* 22) The training also immersed a Spartan into an ideology of communal life that translated on the battlefield into a powerful phalanx of heavy-armed soldiers.

'Education' is too intellectual a term to describe this; 'training' and 'indoctrination' are more accurate. Plutarch writes that Spartan youth learned just enough reading and writing to get by; all the rest was geared towards obedience, hard work and victory (Plutarch, *Lycurgus* 16). Thucydides, writing on classical times, credits his opponent, the Spartan commander Brasidas, with making a pretty good speech 'for a Spartan'. 'Laconic' speech – derived from Laconia, the area in which Sparta is located – describes a terseness of expression that is devoid of rhetorical sophistication, but communicates its message with powerful simplicity. This too was a result of the Spartan *agôgê*, which placed little value on intellectual pursuits, but rather praised quiet pursuit of military virtues. Lycurgus, Plutarch comments, reformed the coinage so that much iron was required for even a little value, but he did the opposite with speech. A few words were expected to carry much meaning.

The process of training began after the elders examined a baby to determine its fitness to survive. Those judged to be inferior were exposed; those who lived were taken, at age seven, into the first of three stages of training. Placed under the control of a *paidonomos*, or child-rearing supervisor, they lived in common barracks, were beaten for infractions, and were hardened to austerity and the discomforts of the weather. They were sent to steal food in the countryside. The system demanded that a tutor – an exemplum, and a disciplinarian – always be on hand for the children, to keep them in line, and to train them for the rigours of Spartan life. The boys were to steal what they needed, from the countryside or from the common messes, and were beaten if they were caught. Put into a position where they would be hungry if they were not successful at procuring their own food, they learned to rely on their own courage and cunning – the very traits they would later need for military life. By keeping the boys from eating too much, the Spartans thought that they would be encouraged to grow tall – as pregnant women who purged themselves were thought to produce healthy children.

This military way of life continued through life. Spartan males were segregated into barracks as adults, and ate common meals apart from families (the *syssitia*, another custom found on Crete). The Spartan order extended to all aspects of life. Strong children, for instance, were a benefit to Sparta – so the Spartans practised a form of eugenics. Spartans thought that prolonged separation of couples, which increased their desire for one another, would lead to healthier children, so Spartan men lived apart from their wives. Sparta even had a *krupteia* – a secret police – that used young men to keep a constant eye on the countryside, and to kill those *helots* who showed any possibility of ever posing a threat to Sparta.

The inculcation of these ideas into Spartan life was strengthened by the use of poetry and songs. This carries a close parallel to Tyrtaeus, Thaletas and Lycurgus, who brought a sense of excellence and law to Sparta through poetry and song. The songs were use as stimulants, Plutarch notes, to rouse their spirits and motivate them to action – and to create, in their minds, a point of focus for their sense of excellence and action. This would become an *ethos* for them, a habituated ideal of action and an unwritten law to guide their lives.

Lycurgus' laws

The *Great Rhêtra* subsumed myriad other laws and customs. Plutarch notes that they called at least some of these *'rhetrai'* because they considered them to be oral sayings brought from the god to Sparta. Focusing always on creating good men through education, Lycurgus set out to inculcate a mentality that was opposed to personal wealth. Claims that he had reformed coinage may be anachronistic, but his debasement of gold, and his law that iron was to be the medium of exchange, were intended to weaken the desire for riches among the population, thus bringing (so it is claimed) harmony to the populace. The anti-luxury strain goes further; one *rhêtra* demanded that an axe only should be used to make the roof of a house, and a saw only in making a door. The rough simplicity of the buildings would end any competition for ostentation among the citizenry. Common meals gave everyone the same food, regardless of position, and although greeted with vehement opposition when proposed, were said to have transformed the Spartans into a harmonious group. Lycurgus sits early in a tradition, stretching into the modern day, of blaming strife on an improper desire for material wealth, and of legislating against the acquisition of wealth by the citizens.

Lycurgus, Plutarch also writes, addressed matters of war, forbidding the repeated campaigns against the same enemy, in order to avoid showing that enemy how to defend themselves. Such a complaint was made against King Agesilaus of Sparta in the 370s, who attacked Theban territory repeatedly, and thus showed the Thebans how to break the Spartan battle line and to invade the Peloponnesus itself. It is interesting that the Spartans do not seem to have considered that their continuous warfare against the *helots* might pose the same problem, perhaps because they held the *helots* in contempt, as masters do slaves, and thus considered them to be beneath the status of a legitimate enemy.

Lycurgus left other laws relating to women and family life. Aristotle later accused Sparta of being too lax with the regulation of women, given that their constitution called for such regulation, but Plutarch disagreed with Aristotle, and then left us a sample of Spartan laws regarding women. Unmarried women were subjected to a tough regimen of physical training, including running, discus and javelin throwing and wrestling, all designed so to foster healthy children and the capacity to withstand childbirth. Lycurgus, it is said, tried to eliminate femininity in women, allowing them to parade around naked, to participate in singing and dancing, and to compose songs in praise of excellent people. This was intended to strengthen ambition and to foster rivalry in young men, and to make the young women also proud and ambitious. (Plutarch, *Lycurgus* 14). One of the prime targets of Lycurgus' laws was marriage, which he encouraged by punishing unmarried men for failing to follow the laws. The main point here is that the Spartans saw no limits to the range of the laws attributed to Lycurgus.

To fulfil his educational purpose, Lycurgus is credited with myriad other laws. To rid the children of fear of death, he lifted the ban on burials within the *polis* and near sanctuaries. The goods to be buried with the corpse, the inscriptions on memorials, the time allowed for mourning – everything was to be regulated for the education of the Spartans. Foreign travel was restricted – military operations aside – because of the bad effects foreigners might have on Spartan citizens. Money was made from iron, to eliminate the lust for gold. As Plutarch put it, Lycurgus made so many educational examples that no part of life was immune to his programme. This would shape everyone into his notion of excellence.

Lycurgus' legacy

Like all lawgivers, Lycurgus found himself in a paradoxical position. On the one hand, he brought a set of moral, political and legal rules that everyone must follow. Even if the laws were founded on social distinctions between people in the *polis*, on principle no one could be exempted from the laws. To create and enforce these laws the lawgiver was entrusted with extraordinary powers: the capacity to modify the basic principles of the community as he saw fit, and to which everyone must conform. However, this very power placed the lawgiver above the laws; how else could he have changed the customs that the community had lived under up to this point? By this same authority, the lawgiver could have applied the laws as he wished to particular cases, or even create laws that applied to some cases differently than others. Since the people of the *polis* are not above their own petty concerns, they may have crowded around him, and asked him to do exactly that. This would have returned the *polis* to the state of confusion that Lycurgus had begun with. Or, as Plutarch interprets for Lycurgus, the lawgiver might have looked at his creation, seen that it was good, and wished it to last beyond his own life.

There was only one course of action open to him. He had to obtain an oath from the people to obey the laws – and then he must exit the scene, leaving them alone with the laws. The exile of the lawgiver – the last stage of many of the traditions – is vital to establish the permanence of the laws, for this is the only way to remove the last vestige of human optionality from the laws themselves. Instead of looking up to him as an authority in their particular squabbles, the people will have to look to the laws as the central anchor for the community. In the end Lycurgus did what every good lawgiver must do. His exile – like that of Solon in Athens and many others – forced the people to obey the laws without the force of his personality. This implanted the laws more deeply into the fabric of the society, and places them off-limits to the manipulations of would-be law-changers.

To accomplish this, Lycurgus, the most elevated of these figures, did what Plutarch – a Platonist, and a priest of Apollo – would wish. He asked the oracle at Delphi whether the laws were good. The oracle's answer was affirmative, so he sent the oracle to Sparta, to further legitimate the laws. And then, having reached the proper time for his life to end, he starved himself to death.

The constitution of Sparta was exceedingly long-lasting for the ancient world. Polybius attributed this to its 'mixed' nature, and claimed that various forces were balanced in a way that no single vicious group could destroy the harmony of the *polis*. Yet the verdict of history on Sparta has not been good. Both Plutarch and Thucydides recorded the case of the 2,000 *helots* who distinguished themselves in brave service to Sparta, who were crowned by the Spartans and led through the shrines of the gods in turn – but then vanished, casualties in the annual war that the Spartans waged against their fellow Greeks. The final result was the decline of Spartan society into the fourth century, and its military defeat by Thebes.

Chapter 6

Solon of Athens

Theseus and early Athens

The Athenians gave credit for their founding to several venerable figures, who were myth-historical in nature. Myths were centred on Erechtheus, with a cult on the Acropolis and related to the god Poseidon, and closely associated with Erichthonius, who was only later distinguished as his grandfather. Erechtheus is mentioned by Homer (*Iliad* 2.546-51) as belonging to a specific *deme* in Attica (a local area, later an administrative unit), and connected to the sacrifice of bulls and rams on the acropolis under the auspices of the goddess Athena. Other figures from Athens' legendary past include Cecrops and Codrus. Such myths presented the people of Athens as 'sprung from the soil' of Attica (*autochthonic*), which Herodotus repeats when he relates the Persian occupation of the Acropolis (8.55). Such stories legitimated Athenian claims to have been the original – and permanent – inhabitants of Attica. Other figures, such as Ion, were introduced to Athens in order to solve specific problems, some were said to have divided the people of Attica into four tribes.

Theseus is the first figure for whom important political enactments were claimed. He cannot be historically dated, and this timeless aspect of his figure is part of his mythological identity. The historian Diodorus (book 4), the biographer Plutarch, and mythographers such as Apollodorus presented him as performing labours similar to those of Heracles, thus connecting the founding of Athens to an heroic past, and elevating Theseus to heroic status. Apollodorus says succinctly, at the end of his stories of Heracles, that during this time Theseus 'cleared the Isthmus of malefactors' (*Library* 2.6.4); Apollodorus later summarizes these deeds (*Epitome* 1.1-24). Such stories could have allowed later Athenians to legitimate their constitution and their laws by associating them with a venerable hero, who, they claimed, brought order to a previously lawless countryside.

Aristotle (or his student) in the *Constitution of the Athenians* gives Theseus a place in Athens' constitutional history, right after the settlement by Ion. Theseus here recognized the need to unify the people of Attica in a *sunoikism* (literally a 'living together', or political union), under a common set of religious rituals, customs and laws. In Plutarch's view, Theseus ended the violent strife between the various parties in Attica by 'forming in his mind a great and wonderful design'. He divided the people into three tribes (the nobles, the farmers and the craftsmen), brought the civic festivals of Oschophoreia (the Rural Dionysia), the Panatheneia and the Metoikeia, to Athens, and thereby united the city and the country politically. Plutarch has a strong tendency to be anachronistic; he also credits Theseus with coining money and establishing a 'democracy', both practices historically later than Theseus could have lived. But the creation of a single political union out of many the many interests in Attica did occur, even if it was the result of a long process rather than a single reformer.

The myths of Theseus were likely all from the sixth century or later; the stories of Erechtheus and Erichthonius were earlier. This suggests the need, by the Athenians, to create a single point of focus to legitimate their *polis*. As part of the same process, the Athenians probably placed their existing standards for resolving disputes under the control of select officials, who wrote them and used them, and who became the germ of a lawgiver tradition associated with stable laws and stable procedures for resolving disputes and preventing the rise of tyrants.

Draco

Draco is the first Athenian figure to whom specific laws have been attributed. He is datable to a particular period – 621 BC or thereabouts – even though we do not have any words from him or direct evidence, beyond literary testimony, that he existed. His name means 'snake', and some scholars have speculated that he really represents a snake cult on the Athenian acropolis that was connected to the laws. It is more likely that he was a real person charged with bringing a resolution to the problems in Athens, in particular a political conspiracy by Cylon and the pollution associated with the killing of his co-conspirators. His laws were closely associated with this event, and with rising tensions between the land-owners and the farmers in Attica.

Aristotle increases the mystery surrounding Draco. The *Constitution of the Athenians* places Draco after the earliest constitution in Athens but before Solon. The *Constitution*'s summary section 41 provides eleven stages of constitutional development in Athens, places Draco between stages two (Theseus) and three (Solon), but does not afford him a stage of his own. Several explanations are possible. One is that Draco was inserted into the text by an editor at a later time, who wanted to represent the traditions that had grown about Draco in the work. But, it is also possible that Aristotle did not ascribe *constitution-maker* status to Draco, but rather the status of a *lawgiver*.

Given this interpretation, Draco (or a group of people collected under his name) enacted legislation – in other words, made *thesmoi*, decrees to be followed as laws – that were in agreement with existing norms and procedures in Athens. He made no fundamental changes to the organiza-tion of the tribes and institutions in Athens, and he offered no deeper norms of *ethos* upon which the society of Athens was founded; he rather put into writing norms that already existed but needed clarification. These were especially murder laws, which were needed to prevent the kinds of long-term feuds that could develop from killings. By writing down existing standards, Draco was participating in a tradition of conservatism that the later Athenians would one day apply to his own laws.

In 409/8 BC the Athenians did just that; they reinscribed the homicide law of Draco, thus looking back into their own past to find a venerable source for their own laws. In this, the only extant inscribed murder law with any detail, the decision to prosecute still rests largely with the families, who will pursue their desire for vengeance. But once charges have been made by a public proclamation in the agora, the law protects the accused from revenge until a decision is reached. This part of the law may be translated, after some restoration, as:

> If anyone slays a murderer or is responsible for his death while he avoids the markets and games and Amphictyonic rites he shall be liable to the same punishment as someone who kills an Athenian.

More generally, Draco's laws are interpreted by Plutarch in his *Life of Solon* 17.2-4:

> One penalty would apply to all almost all offenders: death; so that those convicted of idleness were to be executed, and those who stole vegetables or fruit would be treated the same as temple-robbers or murderers. As a result, Demades [a fourth-century orator] made an impact when he said that Draco wrote his laws in blood. They say that Draco himself, when asked why death was to be the penalty for nearly all offences, answered that small offences deserved it, and he knew of no greater penalty for big offences.

Perhaps Draco hoped to end conflicts in Athens by returning the *polis* to more rigorous enforcement of those existing norms, a move that would have strengthened the hereditary aristocracy. Yet this murder law is an important development, for it gives jurisdiction over a murder case to public institutions, while preventing private individuals from simply taking vengeance on the accused. This would have subordinated an individual's desire for revenge to a public authority. Anyone who refused to go along with the decision would be at odds with the entire community.

In writing the laws Draco brought some stability to judgements, by limiting the discretion available to officials, and by placating those who wanted strong customary laws enforced. This might have reduced disputes over the meaning of the laws, but it would not have rectified the basic injustices embedded into the ancient norms. A bad law, clearly understood and enforced consistently, is still a bad law – especially so if it condones debt slavery. What Athens needed was not a mere writing of existing laws, but a deeper reform to how they dealt with one another.

Solon's social and political reforms

Homer's scene on the Shield of Achilles has two disputants calling upon a man of wisdom to stand between them and bring some satisfaction to their conflict. The dispute is threatening to engulf the entire community. Solon in his poem 36 presented a similar scene to his audience. The city has fallen into lawlessness caused by conflicts, injustice and slavery, and Solon defends his actions by saying:

> On account of these things, making a defence in all directions,
> I stood, as a wolf among many hounds. (Solon 36.26-7)

This scene might represent a microcosm of the conditions in Athens in the generation after Draco, a chaotic, anarchic social crisis that threatened to spread into violence. For one thing, farmers were being taken into slavery for non-payment of their barter debts. To resolve these problems, the people of Athens called upon Solon, a man beholden to none of the disputants, who was able to stand in the middle as chief archon or official in the city and bring a solution acceptable to all. His reputation may have come from urging the people of Athens to fight for control of the island of Salamis, contrary to a law that forbade such incitement.

Contrary to Lycurgus and Theseus, Solon was certainly a real person. The date of his archonship, 594 BC, is supported by many sources, and is our first confirmed date for the early history of Athens. There are many chronological problems associated with him; tradition has placed him in the company of King Croesus of Lydia (who fell in 547 BC), the Pharaoh Amasis of Egypt (who probably came to power in 570 BC) and Pisistratus of Athens, all decades removed from his archonship. Either he was a very young leader (not impossible but highly unlikely), or the tradition associated with him has changed. Herodotus and other writers might have done this to bolster his position as a moral example to the audience, and it reflected through the Greek tradition into Plutarch's *Life of Solon*. This makes many details of his life, and his actions in Athens, very difficult to verify.

But that Solon existed and had a profound affect on Athens is not in doubt. He has left some 270 lines of poetry, priceless records of his own thoughts about matters of life, justice, fate, and the need for a good frame of mind (*noos*) as the foundation for Good Order (*Eunomia*). His poems, and the traditions associated with his laws, do not tell us the same things. While the poems speak of *hubris* (arrogant assaults), the debilitating effects of wealth on a person with a bad frame of mind, the civil strife that follows from such assaults, and his own attempts to bring order to Athens, he leaves us no actual laws. Solon addressed the problems of the *polis* at the deepest levels of human *ethos*, all the while leaving a rich tradition that led later Greeks to identify many written laws with him.

His social and political reforms, according to the tradition, broke the link between aristocratic birth and holding office, and based offices on merit (wealth) rather than family. He organized the citizens into four property classes: the *pentakosiomedimnoi*, or the five hundred bushel men, who could produce that much; the *hippeis*, who could afford a horse; the *zeugetaia* and the *thêtes*. The top two classes held the major offices; the *zeugetaia* could hold minor offices; the *thêtes* could hold no office, but could attend meetings of the citizen assemblies. In this way he mediated the demands of the various parties. The noble families kept control of the highest offices; the common folk could participate in the assemblies, limit the power of the nobles, and most of all participate in juries. It is also said that he created a second council to balance the ancient aristocratic Council of the Areopagus, but this is impossible to verify.

Solon is often credited with having established the Athenian democracy. This is an overstatement – there was nothing akin to a citizen assembly with final authority over the *polis* – but he did lay the general background for the later democratic reforms. Aristotle often speaks of certain measures as 'most democratic', and he blamed Solon in particular for allowing the democratic jury-courts to assert control. This ultimately placed the *polis* under the influence of *demagogues* – orators who would lead the people, often into calamity. But Solon's reforms should be taken as relative to what went on earlier. *Constitution of the Athenians* 9 makes clear that Solon should not be blamed for what went on after his time.

Solon is said to have cancelled the debts that had allowed rich lenders to take poor farmers into slavery. This is his famous *seisachtheia*, or 'shaking-off of burdens', but rather than debt reduction it is more likely that poor farmers, the so-called *hektêmeroi* or 'sixth-parters', were freed from having to turn over a portion of their crops to rich owners. They now had complete rights to the land they worked, and anyone who tried to take a poor farmer into slavery could not use the law to enforce his claim. In a poem Solon speaks of tearing up the boundary stones that had once enslaved the earth; 'earlier she was enslaved, now she is free' (Solon 36.7). Again, what this really means is cryptic; stones were used, in later centuries, as mortgage markers, but this is anachronistic for Solon's time. They could indicate areas, set aside for public use, that individuals had claimed for private use, or most likely they refer to claims placed on private farms which Solon invalidated. In any event, he made no one really happy; the rich wanted to be able to demand payments from enslaved farmers, and the farmers wanted redistribution of all land from the proper owners. Solon stood in the middle and refused to do either.

Claims that he had established new rates of exchange between coins are anachronistic; it is only later that coinage comes into use. He may have put in place a new festival calendar, thus defining the religious celebrations at the heart of *polis* life, and perhaps calling upon the Cretan religious figure Epimenides to purify Athens. Reforms of weights and measures are also credited to him; perhaps he tried to clarify and standardize existing measures.

Justice and moderation

Solon put in place several elements crucial to the rule of law. The first is a general respect for justice, connected to a proper *ethos* in each person, and to a state of mind that disavowed assaults on others and the slavery of Greek men. One of his key concerns is *hubris*, an 'arrogant assault' that follows when a person is unable to moderate his own actions as *dikê* (justice) requires. In a lawful community, each person must act in ways consistent with *dikê,* else the community collapses into disorder or even violence. As Solon says in a fragment of a poem, his so-called *Hymn to the City* (preserved in Demosthenes 19.254f.):

The citizens themselves by their foolishness desire
to destroy the great city, persuaded by material goods,

and the leader of the people has an unbalanced mind, by which
   they are about to suffer many pains from great *hubris*. (Solon 4.5-8)

The result of such *hubris* is to spread violence throughout the community,
which falls prey to factional fighting and slavery when it fails to protect
'the sacred foundations of Justice':

> [*Hubris*] awakens civil strife and sleeping tribal war,
>   which destroys the beautiful youth of many;
> and from its troubles the much-loved city is swiftly
>   worn out, friendships destroyed in unjust factions.
> These evils turn on the people; and of the poor
>   many are brought into foreign lands,
> sold, bound in miserable chains. (Solon 4.17-25)

Solon's alternative to this rapacious violence is *Eunomia*, 'Good Order'
or even 'Lawfulness', as the proper condition of the city. Of this he says:

> These things my heart prompts me to teach the Athenians:
>   how Lawlessness brings the worst evils to the city,
> and Lawfulness manifests good order and everything perfect,
>   and often puts chains on the evil-doers.
> It smoothes what is rough; quells anger, dims *hubris*
>   and shrivels the flowering bud of arrogant destruction.
> It straightens crooked judgements, calms
>   overbearing deeds, stops the deeds of civil strife,
> and stops the anger of grievous strife. It is by this
>   that all things to men are perfect and reach their peak.
>   (Solon 4.30-9)

This is of course not a written law, but rather the state of obedience to
the laws that is a precondition to any laws at all. Solon as a 'wisdom
poet' was considered to be one of the Seven Sages of Greece, who
brought ideas of justice to his fellows and became one of their most
important teachers. In doing so, Solon may have firmly connected the
condition of the *polis* to the condition of each person's *psyche*, his soul
if you will, which would have made it necessary for later thinkers to
develop theories of the soul in order to ground their ideas about the
polis in human nature.

Solon's laws and his legacy

Solon's next major innovation for Athens was to provide the city with written laws, applied similarly to men of all social standings, in a way that would bring violence under control. Solon claims that he had done this in a poem in which he defends his own actions (poem 36 West, preserved in *Constitution of the Athenians* 12.4):

> Many men I brought up to their divinely-founded
> fatherland, men sold, one illegally,
> another legally, and others fleeing
> by forcible necessity, no longer speaking an Attic-tongue,
> as men wandering everywhere;
> and others holding a shameful slavery,
> now trembling before their masters,
> I set them free. By my own power,
> fitting together force with justice,
> these things I did, and I came through as I promised.
> And statutes alike to the base man and to the noble
> fitting straight justice onto each man's case,
> these I wrote. (Solon 36.8-20)

There are many important ideas here: for instance, that Athens was divinely founded, but that her people were often sold into slavery if not run into exile, by a 'forcible necessity' that could mean a creditor coming to enforce his claims. To end these injustices, Solon used his own power, given to him as archon, by which he linked the use of force to justice, as he had said he would. This implies that force would be 'joined harmoniously' to justice, in which the force available to strong men would be placed under the control of just decisions, but also that the decisions of a judge would be enforced. Athens was moving away from the Homeric idea that proper resolutions would require the agreement of both parties, to an enforced decision by judges who act as the laws require. In Solon's own words, Solon's written laws were designed to be applied alike to each person's individual cases.

This last is an important point about the lawgiver's laws. They serve as a set of immutable standards and the point of focus for justice in a just *polis*. But individual cases require flexibility; it is not possible to specify the particular details involved in each case. The judge needs some flexibility, but not too much. Some people claimed that Solon had intentionally made his laws too loose, so that his own friends could judge cases as they wished, and get rich in the process, or perhaps so that the people could take over through their jury decisions. But the *Constitution of the Athenians* has a better answer: that it is not possible to define the best in any particular case in general terms. In any event, Solon must be judged according to his own time, not by what happened later.

Solon's next reform – perhaps the most important of his innovations, an issue of deep importance to the development of law – is his recognition of the fully public nature of his laws. Since individual; injustices can spread into violence across the entire *polis*, disputes between individual persons are not purely their own concerns. Solon is credited with allowing not just the parties to an injustice, but *ho boulomenos* – whoever wishes – to bring a suit. As it developed in later Athens, anyone who wished could challenge an official after his term ended, and anyone could charge another person with murder, not merely the family.

Solon is also credited with having established the right to jury appeal, an important step towards limiting the power of magistrates; any litigant who disagreed with a judge's decision could take his case to a jury of fellow citizens. The ancient Council of the Areopagus would remain the guardians of the laws – to prevent their being changed by over-zealous or dishonest judges or the people in assembly – while the people would have the final say over the decisions in a particular case. We cannot know how far such reforms actually went in Solon's own time. But it is clear that he established a vital precedent: that the decision of judge may itself be judged, against a standard of justice that is written into laws.

For what Solon's own laws actually were, however, we have to trust the testimony of later commentators. We are told that his laws were written on *axones* and *kubreis*, stones or rotating wooden panels that were set up in public display, in the agora or on the acropolis. They probably existed through the sixth century, including the reign of Pisistratus and his sons, and up to the sack of Athens by the Persians in 480 BC. Such displays were created at the very outset of public writing, in archaic characters and doubtless in ways that many – perhaps most – people could not actually read. This is less important than the very fact of their display, and the enormous implications for placing such norms into an objective form, viewable by those participating in *polis* life, and thus not relegating them to the memory and interpretation of a chosen few. These displays may have existed through the fifth century only as copies, and perhaps not in a well-maintained state. In the last years of the fifth century, when the Athenians reinscribed their laws, it was primarily the laws of Solon they returned to. In the fourth century, there was a renewed interest in Solon, who appears in oratory as an authority from the past.

Plutarch cites a law of Solon, which he claims is recorded exactly, in the 'thirteenth table' of his laws. Plutarch implies that there was a set number of tables, with some degree of organization, and that the content of these tables was in some way preserved into the first century AD at least. It is not possible to reconstruct the organization of the laws, but this is one that Plutarch credits to Solon:

> Of those who had lost citizen-rights, those who lost them prior to the archonship of Solon are to regain their rights except those who were convicted by the Areopagus Council, the Magistrates assigned to murder cases, or the king-archons, of homicide, murder or tyrannical ambitions, and had already gone into exile when the law was made. (Plutarch, *Solon* 19).

This law supports Solon's claims, in poem 36 above, that he had returned many of those exiled, living apart from Attica and speaking a foreign tongue, to their proper status at home.

Among the strangest of his laws is the so-called non-neutrality law. In a time of civic strife, when the *polis* is threatened with factional violence, everyone must chose a side. Anyone who refuses to do so must suffer disenfranchisement from political life. Plutarch (*Solon* 20) offers a moral explanation for this, that Solon wished to inculcate a feeling of duty towards one's *polis*, and to eliminate feelings of private separation from affairs of the *polis*. The *Constitution of the Athenians* (8.5) rather claims that the city was often in strife due to apathy, and wanted to eliminate the strife by ending the apathy. In either case, it is a strange law, which suggests strong differences between our own laws and those of the Greek past.

Solon makes no mention of women in his poems, but there are several laws recorded in his name that regulate the conduct of women. An heiress, Plutarch claims, may sleep with a close relative of her husband should he be impotent; this might have been to keep the property within the family, although Plutarch again bolsters Solon's position as a moral legislator, crediting him with wanting to prevent estrangement between couples. Solon is also said to have abolished dowries by ending the transfer of property at the time of marriage; this was an attempt to preserve the wealth in existing estates, and prevent the impoverishment of landed families. He may also have regulated women with laws requiring neatness while outdoors and in mourning, and with laws concerning adultery and seduction. He made, we are told, an exception for prostitutes, who do not disguise their actions. Solon is even said to have established state-sanctioned houses of prostitution. Sons born out of wedlock, Plutarch also claims, need not support their fathers; the father has already made their birth into something shameful. Solon also changed wills, to make land alienable from the family if there are no children, as long as the person making the will was not under bad influences, such as the persuasion of a woman. All of these laws are immersed in Plutarch's own ideas of propriety and morality.

Solon is credited with many laws that fostered Athens' transition into a trading economy. He is credited with banning all exports except olive oil; Plutarch places this law on 'the first of his tables' (24). Solon made laws to regulate wells, the planting of trees, and biting dogs. Publicly funded meals were his concern too; he made it illegal for one person to be fed repeatedly at public expense, since (according to Plutarch) this fostered greed. This last is quite different from Lycurgus in Sparta, who, concerned to create a citizen *ethos* based on communal events and solidarity against common enemies, made such meals central to public life. Solon, however, is said to have made it illegal to turn down the opportunity to eat at public meals, since such refusal showed contempt for the *polis*.

Here is an example of how Solon was used by orators in fourth-century Athens to attack their enemies. The orator Demosthenes wrote a speech against one Timocrates, accused of proposing an unconstitutional law, in which the speaker says the following:

> The statutes of Solon, surely a lawgiver very different from this man [Timocrates], said that a man convicted of theft shall be imprisoned if he is not executed; that anyone who mistreats his parents shall go to jail if seen in the marketplace; and that anyone convicted of avoiding military service shall go to jail if he acts as if he had citizen rights. Timocrates absolves all such men from prison, if they pay bail. (Demosthenes xxiv, *Against Timocrates* 103)

Demosthenes then calls for nothing less than Timocrates' execution. In a few words, Demosthenes links Timocrates with theft, parental abuse, draft-dodging, corrupting the marketplace, polluting the idea of citizenship, and coddling criminals. Clearly it is the name of Solon that lends weight to the speaker's argument, not the accuracy of the citation of the law.

In the end, Solon's laws developed out of a tradition that revered him as the figure of justice at the fountainhead of the Athenian system of self-government. In terms not inconsistent with his own words in his poem 36, when he had pleased no one with his reforms and the people gathered around him 'as a wolf in a pack of hounds', he is said to have done what was credited to many lawgivers. He swore the people of Athens to follow the laws (the tradition differs as to whether this was for ten or a hundred years), and then he went into exile. He travelled the Mediterranean, engaging in his *theôria*, or examination of the world, by sightseeing in Egypt, Asia Minor, Crete and Cyprus. He may have gone back to Athens, and perhaps his reforms should be divided into two parts, those before his travels and those after. Solon's own verses opposing tyranny may have been sung late in his life, and in response to the tyrant Pisistratus. Herodotus credits Solon with bringing a law back from the Pharaoh Amasis of Egypt, requiring everyone to declare annually his source of livelihood, and thus to encourage industriousness. Plutarch places Solon with Pisistratus, perhaps in the late 560s, which would have made Solon young when he carried out the first stage of his reforms in the 590s, and older when he saw the rise of Pisistratus into tyrannical rule over Athens. Despite these uncertainties of chronology, that Solon was the premier lawgiver in Athens' history is beyond doubt.

Chapter 7

Lesser Known Lawgivers

There are many lawgiver figures of lesser renown – at least to us – than Lycurgus and Solon. Some of them may have lived earlier than these more well-known figures, and were perhaps just as innovative. Each would have been extremely influential in his particular community, or even more widely, were his laws adopted in other areas. In general they cannot be established historically outside of the reports of the literary sources, and we have almost no details of their lives.

In addition to those discussed below, there are others of whom we know little apart from their names: Diocles in Syracuse, Aristides of Ceos, Pheidon of Corinth (who may have passed his laws to Philolaus), Demonax in Cyrene, and one Onomacritus, perhaps a Locrian. Of the latter, Aristotle (*Politics* 2.12) notes that some say Onomacritus was a friend of Thaletas of Crete, that Lycurgus and Zaleucus heard Onomacritus speak, and that Charondas heard Zaleucus (Strabo 6.1). This would give Onomacritus an important place in the transmission of laws – but Aristotle discounts all of this as being chronologically impossible. Aristotle also considers a connection between the laws of Androdamus of Rhegium and the Chalcidians in Thrace.

The most important literary source for these figures is in the second book of Aristotle's *Politics*, especially section 12, but some of them appear in law-court speeches of fourth-century Athens, and in the later historical tradition, especially the historians Polybius and Diodorus of Sicily. There are aspects of *polis* life associated with them that suggest a role for early Greek lawgivers that was wider than the creation of laws as we know them. As mentioned earlier, Aristotle himself categorizes them; some wrote laws and constitutions, and others wrote laws only. Each of these figures can be used to illustrate a particular aspect of early Greek law – and that is the approach taken here.

Zaleucus of Locris

Locris, a town in southern Italy, is most fully known as Locri Epizephyrii, to distinguish it from Locris on mainland Greece. It was founded as a colony of the Opuntian Locrians, from the area of Boiotia, in the seventh century BC. Locris was ruled by an hereditary aristocracy, and its laws would have been designed to maintain the rule of an aristocratic elite. Later writers tell us that the lawgiver Zaleucus provided the town with one of the earliest written law lists (it is not extant today). According to Aristotle, this puts him, along with Charondas and Philolaus, in the class of lawgivers who wrote laws for foreign cities.

One tradition surrounding Zaleucus sees him as a conservative: creating harsh laws, which he intended to be kept without changes, and which had the divine sanction of the gods. This strongly suggests an aristocratic background. Yet his social origin is also suggested to have been that of a shepherd who brought, in simple austerity, laws to his community. He is thus afforded an origin outside of the aristocracy, akin to Lycurgus, Solon and Charondas, yet he intends to maintain the aristocratic prerogatives. The first-century BC historian Diodorus disagrees with this, attributing noble birth to Zaleucus, as well as an education.

Zaleucus, according to tradition, brought the laws to the Locrians by way of an oracle, a claim also made for Lycurgus. Such claims to divine sanction are common for *poleis* with aristocratic governments, who are concerned with maintaining the position of the aristocracy as the guardians of the laws and the final authority. To do this they claim an ancient lineage for themselves, and for their town, thus linking their way of doing things to both their ancestors and the gods; thus some said that Zaleucus got his laws from Thaletas of Crete. Such traditions may be claiming a connection to ancient Crete more than accurately reconstructing Zaleucus' activities. It is more likely that his laws were independent, or drew upon Greek sources that were commonly understood rather than specific laws in a specific place. In any case, Zaleucus' purpose in bringing the laws was practical, to alleviate turmoil, a common motif for lawgivers, who confront real dangers in their communities. Having received his laws from Athena in a dream, say some, he was appointed *nomothetês*, the establisher of laws.

He is credited with many laws (*nomoi*) having prescribed penalties (Ephorus, *FGrH* 70F139), a claim also made for Charondas of Catana. His most important innovation may be that of limiting the authority of judges and thus stabilizing the administration of judgements through fixed remedies. One later writer, Aelian, claims that he made a law requiring adulterers to be blinded (*Varia Historia* 13.24), a law which would have contrasted with the punishment alleged to exist in Cumae, which was to walk around the *polis* for three days bound with ropes (Plutarch, *Greek Questions* 2). Like many such figures, the passage of time has magnified, and distorted, our information about him; Diodorus, who considers him a student of the philosopher Pythagoras, also calls upon later philosophical views in attributing Zaleucus with laws requiring people to believe in a *kosmos* that is the orderly creation of the gods, in order to keep men's souls pure (Diodorus 12.20).

Charondas of Catana

Catana, a town on the east coast of Sicily, north of Syracuse and south of Messana, was a Greek colony from the Chalcidice, in the northern Aegean Sea. The area around Sicily was politically and militarily turbulent, being at the nexus of struggles between Carthage (originally a colony of the Phoenicians on Africa), Syracuse, and other Greek cities, such as Sybaris, Croton and Thurii. Catana was founded in the middle of the eighth century BC, *c.* 750, as part of the colonization movement that spread Greek culture to the west. The cultural influences included Greek ideas of law and politics, trade and friendship connections, as well as philosophical schools associated with Pythagoras and others. Pythagoras may have written laws for the city of Croton, although the evidence is slim. The later historian Diodorus is himself influenced by neo-Pythagoreanism, he credits Charondas, for example, with a law requiring all sons of citizens to learn to read, from teachers paid publicly (12.12-13).

Charondas was the lawgiver credited with writing laws for his native Catana, probably in the late seventh century BC. Details about him and his laws are less than sketchy, and subject to the mutations of a literary tradition. It is probable, however, that his influence was wider than Catana, given the spread of his laws to other cities on Sicily and southern Italy, in particular the Chalcidic Greek colonies – Naxos, Zancles, Mylae, Himera, Rhegium and Cyme, and even east to Mazaka in Cappadocia. Rhegium, for instance, on the toe of Italy, may have received its laws from Catana, and evidence, particularly coinage, suggests that it maintained stronger connection to the cities on Sicily than on Italy (see Graham, *Colony and Mother City,* 17-18). Aristotle mentions a lawgiver, Andro-damas of Rhegium, nowhere else cited, who he says made laws regarding murder and heiresses for the Chalcidians of Thrace, which would also connect Rhegium to the Chalcidice in the northern Aegean area.

Aristotle's *Politics* 2.12 and Diodorus 12.11-18 credit Charondas with highly detailed laws, especially of a family nature. For instance, he precluded a man who brought home a stepmother for his children from publicly deliberating in his fatherland, since he had planned so badly for his own family (12.12). He also had a law regarding heiresses (12.18).

Other laws are alleged to include one requiring a person who had falsely accused another to wear a wreath of tamarisk, as a prize for wickedness; another required a coward in war to dress as a woman and sit in the town's market for three days (12.16). It is highly unlikely that such laws are historically accurate – we are reading a literary tradition, not accurate records or reconstruction – yet the tradition is probably right to attribute such a breadth of concern to his laws.

Along with Zaleucus, Charondas may have tried to bring more precision to the administration of the laws in procedures as well as penalties. Aristotle cites a procedural law that allowed a notice of an intent to prosecute in suits for false witness. Aristotle writes that in the accuracy (*akribeia*) of his laws, Charondas was even more finished than modern legislators (*Politics* 2.12, 1274b5-8).

Charondas and other lawgivers on Italy may have been extremely influential in spreading Greek laws across the central Mediterranean. Even many Romans later thought that Greek laws had been brought to Rome; the story of an embassy from Rome to Athens under the Roman decemvirs, when the Romans wrote their so-called Twelve Tables (mid-fifth century), was accepted by Dionysius of Halicarnassus (*Roman Antiquities* 10.51f.) and Livy (3.31). Cicero, in his *On Laws* 2.25.64, thought that a law of Solon had been imported to Rome.

Phaleas of Chalcedon

Phaleas is known for one thing only: the first constitution based on fully-fledged egalitarianism of property, meaning an equality of farm lots. Nothing meaningful is known about whether his constitution was ever actually enacted. Aristotle, *Politics* 2.12, finds the equalization of possessions to be a first for Phaleas, and unique to him, although it is later seen in idealized form in Plato's *Republic* (Aristotle's criticism is at 2.5). Aristotle leaves a brief summary in 2.7 of how equality of possessions and its influence on a community was recognized by various lawgivers and their laws. Various approaches include (1) Solon's legislation, which rejected such equality, all the while addressing gross discrepancies and forbidding debt slavery; (2) laws which set limits to real property; (3) the law of Locris, which bans the sale of property; and (4) the laws of entail – which set limits to inheritances – for example at Leucas, where the failure to use the laws led the constitution to become an extreme democracy.

Aristotle's description of Phaleas focuses almost exclusively on his goal of equalizing property, and says nothing about how that was to be achieved or how the people could be brought to accept such a plan. It seems unlikely that Phaleas himself would have ignored these matters; it is probable, rather, that Aristotle did not see them as necessary to his own criticism of Phaleas' constitution. In particular, there is nothing on Phaleas' view of education, whereby people might be persuaded to accept such a proposal, and nothing about the ethical norms needed to sustain such a constitution. This strikes to the heart of how a philosopher such as Plato or Aristotle approached the matter, through the moral character of the citizens, for this determines the basic character of a city. If the desires of the citizens do not match the lawgiver's plan for property, then the plan will not work.

To establish such egalitarianism in a new *polis* would be difficult, for those directing the project will have taken greater risks and want greater rewards; no one would easily accept an outright confiscation and redistribution of land. Phaleas' plan was to do it through the regulation of dowries – land transfers during marriages. The rich would receive no dowries, but would pay them; the poor would pay none, but would receive them. As a result, wealth would, through marriages, flow to the less affluent. This plan contrasts with the approach of Philolaus (below) because their projects are different. Phaleas wants to equalize farm holdings, and must thus redistribute wealth in a way that people will accept; Philolaus wants to freeze existing allotments.

In the end, ancient commentators concluded that Phaleas had failed to recognize the importance of matters other than property – for instance, the need to avoid tyranny and to provide for military defence. If accounts are accurate, his own inability to consider the implications of his property laws prevented him from offering a fuller description of how such a plan would actually work. But this limitation upon Phaleas may be an accident of preservation.

Philolaus of Corinth

Philolaus ('friend of the people') was a member of the leading family in Corinth, the Bacchiads. (He must not be confused with the Pythagorean philosopher Philolaus of Croton, a contemporary of Socrates.) Aristotle, in his account at *Politics* 2.12, 1274b1f., writes that Philolaus of Corinth moved to Thebes as the lover of an Olympic victor, one Diocles, who hated the amorous passions of his mother. The story that a rich man might give up his wealth and position to move to Thebes for this reason was perhaps originally intended to strengthen the prestige of Thebes, often an enemy of Corinth. Plutarch, in his *Life of Pelopidas* 19 (Pelopidas was a fourth-century Theban general), considers a similar story but claims that its origin is in the emigration of early lawgivers, who needed to quiet the violent passions of the Thebans in order to foster order. To do so they relied on reforms of music, especially the flute. A true reformer of the constitution would certainly introduce the people to musical habits designed to calm their emotions; a similar tradition is attached to Thaletas of Crete, for instance, whom Lycurgus of Sparta may have sent to Crete to bring calm through his songs (pseudo-Plutarch, *de Musica* 9.1134c).

Historically, and leaving the story of love aside, we may conclude that when the people of Thebes needed outside help to reform their laws, they called upon Philolaus, who came in as a neutral third party. In distinction from many of the early lawgivers, he was said by Aristotle to have ended his life in Thebes, not in exile. He is among those, Aristotle wrote, who fashioned laws for a foreign city, not his own.

Philolaus of Corinth and Phaleas of Chalcedon likely faced the same issue: the need to maintain order in the city and minimize the effects of factions by stabilizing land allotments. It is in family law – meaning, here, laws for the regulation of family wealth – that Philolaus may have focused. There was likely a social crisis that resulted from a degradation of family farm holdings, probably a need to prevent the division of land among heirs, or through marriages. Aristotle claims that Philolaus made laws relating to the begetting of children, which the Thebans probably called 'adoption' laws, but which may have allowed the creation of wills for the preservation of estates ('testation'). With his family laws, Philolaus may have tried to keep a fixed number of farms in place, perhaps as a means to prevent the progressive weakening or aggrandizement of farm lots. That this is the only law we have from Philolaus may also be a matter of preservation.

Philolaus illustrates the Greek view that the laws may be used to regulate matters of the *oikos* – in particular, allotments of land – as a means to stabilizing the *polis* itself. In his criticism of Plato's *Laws* in *Politics* 2.6, and at 2.7, Aristotle makes several comments about this practice, in passages dealing with the egalitarianism of property expounded by Phaleas. Such laws may have been part of a general movement towards regularizing civic life and correcting unjust practices from the past. The Thebans, for instance, may have already made it illegal to expose a child, rather allowing the father to sell it through a magistrate, after which it became a slave (Aelian, *Varia Historia* 2.7).

Pittacus of Mytilene

All the lawgivers so far could boast of popular support, and were often called in to solve a crisis. None appears to have seized and held power by force alone, which is the action of a tyrant. A tyrant in ancient Greece was not necessarily brutal, and he might bring prosperity and order to a *polis*, but he did seize power outside customary or constitutional procedures. Yet certain of these early figures skirt the line between legitimate lawgiver and tyrant, acting at times with force to keep the citizens in line for the sake of their power, and at other times demonstrating their legitimacy by maintaining order in a proper sense.

One such type was the *aisumnêtês*, or elective tyranny, which Aristotle describes as an office that is in one sense elective, or chosen (*hairetê*), by people who are willing to live under a tyrant for the sake of good order, and in another sense tyrannical in that there is a master who uses force to maintain power (*Politics* 3.14). The position exhibits some similarities to the Roman position of *dictator*, a man chosen for a set period of time to alleviate an emergency, yet who holds unlimited power during his appointment (Dionysus of Halicarnassus 5.73). Pittacus of Mytilene was such a person – a man chosen to save his fatherland from an emergency, but also a tyrant known for his brutality. Pittacus was, according to some lists, among the so-called Seven Sages – men known for their wisdom (e.g. Plato, *Protagoras* 343C).

Mytilene is an island in the northern Aegean Sea. Around 590 BC the Mytileneans may have faced political turmoil and a struggle for control. There was likely a serious problem of exiles trying to return, perhaps under the leadership of the poet Alcaeus; such an inundation of people can threaten the stability of the *polis* as well as the positions of the leadership and the people. Pittacus was opposed to Alcaeus. One side might claim that the leaders of the exiles were destroyers of the political order – such a view would reflect badly on Alcaeus. But a fragment of Alcaeus preserved in Aristotle's *Politics* (3.14) maintains the opposite. The people, he sings, 'having made the low-born Pittacus tyrant of the spiritless and unlucky city, all together shout his praises'. Despite the efforts of a returning aristocracy, Pittacus gained control and ruled from 589 to 579 BC.

Pittacus was, according to Aristotle, a maker of laws and not of constitutions. His reforms did not extend to a fundamental reordering of the city; he rather corrected specific deficiencies in the laws. He made a law, for instance, that if a drunken man should commit a crime, he is to pay more than a sober man. The point of the law here would likely relate to the island's position as a producer of wine; if the old law pardoned drunken men, because there were more of them, then Pittacus reversed the policy, and brought the problem under control by more vigorous enforcement. Rather than function by equity – the idea of fairness – which would tend towards leniency for crimes committed by drunkards, Pittacus opted for results. Thus he demonstrates a measure of political pragmatism over idealism, rejecting customary norms if they led to results detrimental to his purposes.

Hippodamus of Miletus

A true constitution-maker crafts a comprehensive order for the *polis*, an arrangement not only of laws but of the norms necessary for life. He arranges not only the rules by which people live, but also the standard of justice by which individual disputes should be judged and individual virtues modelled. For Phaleas, the political order required a certain arrangement of property, intended to minimize conflict. Hippodamus of Miletus is known less for his laws than for a different aspect of arrangement: city planning of streets and buildings, a way of connecting the organization of the *polis* to its physical layout. The connection between such a physical layout and the political constitution and laws may be unfamiliar to us, but it was not so in the ancient world; Polybius, a Greek of the second century BC, who leaves us a history of Rome during the Punic Wars, dedicates his book 6 to Rome's political constitution – including the layout of the Roman military camp.

Hippodamus was born in the fifth century, no earlier than 475 BC – he is thus later than most of the early lawgivers discussed here. He is famous for having designed the layout of the Piraeus, the port of Athens, in the 450s under Pericles; the market-place in the Piraeus was called the Agora of Hippodamus (Xenophon, *Hellenica* 2.4). In 444 he likely directed the rebuilding of Thurii, on Italy, since he was later called a Thurian. Diodorus (12.10) describes three streets running one way, four another; this suggests a Pythagorean connection to the special number seven. He also built the new federal capital on the island of Rhodes, probably in 408 or 406, according to Strabo (14).

In his constitutional and legal proposals, Hippodamus divided his city of 10,000 into three parts: craftsman, farmers and warriors. He then divided the land into thirds: sacred, public and private. The laws were also of three kinds: cases of insolence, injury and death. He also made changes to the way courts decided cases, dividing the decisions into three kinds. The rulers were to be selected by the three parts of the *polis*, and were to take care of three things: foreign affairs, affairs held in common, and orphans. All of this suggests a mathematical basis for his reforms, an attempt to find order in equal divisions of equal amounts. It is plausible that he came into contact with Pythagorean mathematics and philosophy while in Thurii.

These proposals would mesh nicely with his architectural and civic planning work, but would doubtless not work in practice. Aristotle sees Hippodamus as little concerned for the deeper issues of justice. But this may be unfair, for his division of the population into thirds may have been an attempt to mix democracy with oligarchy or aristocracy, and his reforms of the courts may have been intended to subordinate the democratic assembly – always prone to rash if not illegal actions – to the laws as interpreted by the courts. His description of a class of warriors may have been an attempt to avoid the use of mercenaries while creating a profession of arms. It is also true that Hippodamus, by demonstrating less concern for the ethical aspects of the *polis* than for its arrangement and its laws, may have had a new conception of law as positivistic rules rather than an expression of a moral order.

Hippodamus' primary fame remains as an architect and a civic planner. Yet the rational order for streets, markets and buildings that he provided is no small contribution to political life. It reveals the orderly nature of his mind, and would have also had an important effect on the order governing the citizens' lives. Aristotle's *Politics* 7.11 sees his geometric street-plan as very effective for every purpose but one: military defence. An old-fashioned chaotic arrangement was better able to confuse the enemy.

Suggestions for Further Reading

Literary sources

Ancient texts available in Penguin Classics translation include the following:

Homer: *Iliad* and *Odyssey*, tr. R. Fagles (the line numbers differ from standard classical references).
The Homeric Hymns, tr. J. Cashford.
Hesiod: *Theogony / Works and Days*; Theognis: *Elegies*, tr. D. Wender.
Herodotus: *The Histories*, tr. A. de Sélincourt.
Aristotle's *Constitution of the Athenians*, tr. P.J. Rhodes.
Aristotle: *The Politics*, tr. T.A. Sinclair.
Aristotle: *The Art of Rhetoric,* tr. H. Lawson-Tancred.
Aristotle: *The Nicomachean Ethics,* tr. J. Barnes.
Plutarch: *The Age of Alexander*, and *The Rise and Fall of Athens,* tr. I. Scott-Kilvert.
Plutarch: *On Sparta,* tr. R.J.A. Talbert.
Polybius: *The Rise of the Roman Empire,* tr. I. Scott-Kilvert.

These texts are also available in the Loeb Classical Library, published by Harvard University Press, which gives an English translation facing the Greek (or Latin) text. The earlier volumes in this series reflect the translation styles and customs of the late nineteenth or early twentieth century; later volumes are often more literal and thus more spare.

For archaic Greek poets, including Solon, see the Loeb volume edited and translated by D.E. Gerber: *Greek Elegiac Poetry* (Cambridge, MA: Harvard University Press, 1999). The numbering is that of the Greek edition by M.L. West, *Iambi et Elegi Graeci* (Oxford: Clarendon, 1971; re-published by Sandpiper, 1998).
For Plato see *Plato's Complete Works*, edited by J.M. Cooper (Indianapolis: Hackett Publishing, 1997).
In many cases, a fragment preserved in a literary source will also be

available in F. Jacoby's *Fragmente der Griechischen Historiker* (1923-). Advanced students should be aware of these redactions.

Editions of Aristotle's texts and commentaries include:

S. Everson (ed.), *The Politics and The Constitution of Athens* (Cambridge: Cambridge University Press, 1996).

J.M. Moore, *Aristotle and Xenophon on Democracy and Oligarchy* (Chatto and Windus: The Hogarth Press, 1983).

P.L.P. Simpson, *A Philosophical Commentary on the Politics of Aristotle* (Chapel Hill: University of North Carolina Press, 1998).

W.L. Newman, *The Politics of Aristotle* (Oxford: Clarendon, 1887), text and commentary.

F. Susemihl and R.D. Hicks, *The Politics of Aristotle: A Revised Text* (London: Macmillan, 1884).

P.J. Rhodes, *A Commentary on the Aristotelian Athenaiôn Politeia* (Oxford: Clarendon, 1993).

General histories

The first stop for a new topic is *Oxford Classical Dictionary*, 3rd edn, ed. A. Spawforth and S. Hornblower (Oxford: Oxford University Press, 1996).

The volumes of the *Cambridge Ancient History* remain fundamental. Used here are several essays from the 2nd edition, vol. III, part 3.

O. Murray, *Early Greece* (Cambridge, MA: Harvard University Press, 1993), for a narrative history of archaic Greece.

J.M. Hall, *A History of the Archaic Greek World, 1200-479 BCE* (Oxford: Blackwell, 2007) presents some of the problems involved in understanding archaic history.

Volumes in the same series as the present work (Classical World series, published by Bristol Classical Press) dealing with related topics include:

N.R.E. Fisher, *Slavery in Classical Greece* (1993)
S.C. Todd, *Athens and Sparta* (1996)
M. Edwards, *The Attic Orators* (2005)

Modern discussions of Greek law

The literature on Greek law is huge. A few essential works are:

M. Gagarin, *Early Greek Law* (Berkeley: University of California Press, 1989). Perhaps the best short introduction to early Greek law.

R.J. Bonner and G. Smith, *The Administration of Justice from Homer to Aristotle*, vol. 1 (NY: AMS Press, 1970). A seminal study of how the law was administered.

M. Gagarin and D. Cohen (eds), *A Cambridge Companion to Ancient Greek Law* (Cambridge: Cambridge University Press, 2005). Includes chapters on the unity of Greek law and early Greek law (M. Gagarin), writing and laws (R. Thomas), and Greek law and religion (R. Parker).

D. Cohen, *Law, Violence and Community in Classical Athens* (Cambridge: Cambridge University Press, 1995). Connects litigation to the regulation of violence in an agonistic society.

S.C. Todd, *The Shape of Athenian Law* (Oxford: Clarendon, 1993). Deals primarily with classical Athens.

D.M. MacDowell, *The Law in Classical Athens* (Ithaca: Cornell University Press, 1978). The first part deals with the growth a legal system in early Greece, with discussions of primitive disputes, the scene on the Shield of Achilles, and Draco and Solon.

G.M. Calhoun, *The Growth of Criminal Law in Ancient Greece* (Berkeley: University of California Press, 1927). Discusses the growth of criminal, meaning public, law.

A.R. Harrison, *The Law of Athens*, 2 vols (Oxford: Oxford University Press, 1968/1971). Focuses on classical Athens.

J.W. Jones, *The Law and Legal Theory of the Greeks: An Introduction* (Oxford: Oxford University Press, 1956).

E.M. Tetlow, *Women, Crime and Punishment in Ancient Law and Society* (NY: Continuum, 2005).

Epigraphic sources and compilations of laws

C.F. Fornara (ed. and tr.), *Archaic Times to the End of the Peloponnesian War* (Cambridge: Cambridge University Press, 1988). All selections in translation.

I. Arnaoutoglou, *Ancient Greek Laws: A Sourcebook* (London: Routledge, 1998). All in translation.

M. Dillon and L. Garland, *Ancient Greece: Social and Historical Documents from Archaic Times to the Death of Socrates (c. 800-399*

BC), 2nd edn (London: Routledge, 2000). All in translation.

R. Meiggs and D. Lewis, *A Selection of Greek Historical Inscriptions to the End of the Fifth Century BC* (Oxford: Clarendon, 1980) (abbreviated M&L). Scholarly presentation of the Greek texts.

M.N. Tod, *A Selection of Greek Historical Inscriptions to the End of the Fifth Century BC*, 2nd edn (Oxford: Clarendon, 1946) (abbreviated Tod). Scholarly presentation of the Greek texts.

Chapter 1: Approaching Greek Laws and Lawgivers

Chios inscription: M&L no. 8; Tod no. 1; Gagarin, *Early Greek Law*, 89-91; Fornara no. 19.

Eretreia inscription: Gagarin, *Early Greek Law*, 91-3.

Draco's homicide law: M&L 86; Fornara no. 15; Gagarin, *Early Greek Law*, 86-9.

Dreros inscription: M&L no. 2; Fornara no. 11; Gagarin, *Early Greek Law*, 81-2.

R.F. Willetts (ed.), *The Law Code of Gortyn* (Berlin: Walter de Gruyter, 1967). Greek text with translation and commentary.

Demosthenes: speeches 19 *On the False Legation* and 46 *Against Stephanus II* can be found in the Loeb vol. II, translated by C.A. Vince and J.A. Vince, and vol. V, translated by A.T. Murray (Cambridge, MA: Harvard University Press, 1999 and 1990). Solon poem 4 is at Demosthenes 19.251f.

Xenophanes poem no. 1, on poets and athletes, is in the Loeb volume D.E. Gerber (tr.), *Greek Elegiac Poetry* (Cambridge, MA: Harvard University Press, 1999).

Plutarch, *Life of Alexander*, first paragraph, for the statement on biography versus history. Plutarch, *Life of Solon* for the biography of Solon.

M. Lefkowitz, *The Lives of the Greek Poets* (London: Duckworth, 1983) discusses many problems in evaluating the biographical tradition of early Greek poets and thinkers.

For an introduction to early elegiac poetry, see A.W.H. Adkins, *Poetic Craft in the Early Greek Elegists* (Chicago and London: Chicago University Press, 1985).

Chapter 2: Early Greek Order, Justice and Law

For the law-code of Hammurabi, see C. Edwards (tr.), *The Hammurabi Code* (London: Watts, 1921).

On early Greek political thinking, see the essay by K.A. Raaflaub, 'Poets, lawgivers, and the beginnings of political reflection in archaic Greece', in *The Cambridge History of Greek and Roman Political Thought*, ed. C. Rowe and M. Schofield (Cambridge: Cambridge University Press, 2000), 23-59.

On early Greek moral values, see A.W.H. Adkins, *Moral Values and Political Behaviour in Ancient Greece from Homer to the End of the Fifth Century* (London: Chatto and Windus, 1972).

The classic study of *hubris* is N.R.E. Fisher, *Hybris: A Study in the Values of Honour and Shame in Ancient Greece* (Warminster: Aris and Phillips, 1992).

On *themis*, a classic work is J.E. Harrison, *Themis: A Study of the Social Origins of Greek Religion* (Cambridge: Cambridge University Press, 1912). There have been several editions since, including *Epilegomena to the Study of Greek Religions and Themis: A Study of the Social Origins of Greek Religion* (White Fish, Montana, USA: Kessinger Publishing, 2003).

On *Themis* as a goddess: E.J. Stafford, 'Themis: religion and order in the Archaic *polis*', in L.G. Mitchell and P.J. Rhodes (eds), *The Development of the Polis in Archaic Greece* (London: Routledge, 1997), 158-67.

On Greek justice, see R. Sealey, *The Justice of the Greeks* (Ann Arbor: University of Michigan Press, 1994); H. Lloyd-Jones, *The Justice of Zeus* (Berkeley, Los Angeles and London: University of California Press, 1971); E.A. Havelock, *The Greek Concept of Justice: From its Shadow in Homer to its Substance in Plato* (Cambridge, MA and London: Harvard University Press, 1978). Two important articles are by M. Gagarin, '*Dike* in the Works and Days', in *Classical Philology* 68 (1973): 81-94, and '*Dike* in Archaic Greek Thought', in *Classical Philology* 69 (1974): 186-97.

Two classic books on the development of Greek thought are B. Snell, *The Discovery of the Mind: The Origins of European Thought,* T.G. Rosenmeyer (tr.), (Cambridge, Mass: Harvard University Press, 1953), and E.R. Dodds, *The Greeks and the Irrational* (Berkeley: University of California Press, 1951). More recent discussions can be found in J. Brunschwig and G.E.R. Lloyd (eds), *Greek Thought: A Guide to Classical Knowledge* (Cambridge, MA: Harvard University Press, 2000).

3. The Lawgiver and his Laws

For a discussion of Greek versus Near Eastern lawgivers and laws, and on the archaic understanding of law, see E.M. Harris, 'Solon and the spirit of the law in Archaic and Classical Greece', in *Democracy and the Rule of Law in Classical Athens* (Cambridge: Cambridge University Press, 2006), 3-28. Harris compares Deioces with Solon, and observes how the former seized tyrannical power, in contrast to Solon's refusal of it.

On reason in the Greek city: O. Murray, 'Cities of Reason', in O. Murray and S. Price (eds), *The Greek City from Homer to Alexander* (Oxford: Clarendon, 1990), 1-28.

For Antiphon, see the Loeb volume *Minor Attic Orators I: Antiphon, Andokides* (tr. K.J. Maidment, 1953).

On the legends of the lawgivers, see A. Szegedy-Maszak, 'Legends of the Greek lawgivers', in *Greek, Roman and Byzantine Studies* 19 (1978): 199-209.

The oral and written natures of early Greek law is discussed by R. Thomas, 'Written in stone? Liberty, equality, orality, and the codification of law', in L. Foxhall and A.D.E. Lewis (eds), *Greek Law in its Political Setting* (Oxford: Clarendon, 1996): 9-31.

Fragments of the Twelve Tables of Roman Law may be found in the Loeb volume *Remains of Old Latin III: Lucilius, and Laws of the XII Tables* (tr. E.H. Warmington, 1967).

4. Minos and Rhadamanthus of Crete

On Minos, Theseus and the Minotaur: Herodotus 7.170-1; Diodorus Siculus 4.59-63, 76-79; Plutarch, *Life of Theseus*.

R.F. Willetts, 'Cretan laws and society', in *Cambridge Ancient History*, 2nd edn, vol. III, part 3, ch. 39c, 234-48.

S.M. Trzaskoma, R.S. Smith and S. Brunet (ed. and tr.), *Anthology of Classical Myth* (Indianapolis: Hackett Publishing, 2004), 443-6 for an introduction to gods on Linear B tablets.

5. Lycurgus of Sparta

The most important studies of Sparta begin with W.G. Forrest, *A History of Sparta,* 2nd edn (London: Duckworth, 1980), on its early political history.

P.A. Cartledge, *Sparta and Lakonia: a Regional History, 1300-362 BC* (London: Routledge, 1979) is an in-depth discussion of the rise of Sparta.

G.E.M. de Ste Croix, *The Origins of the Peloponnesian War* (London: Duckworth, 1972) has detailed information on the development of Sparta into a leading power.

Very readable is P.A. Cartledge, *The Spartans: The World of the Warrior-Heroes of Ancient Greece* (NY: Vintage Books, 2002/03).

N.G.L. Hammond, 'The Peloponnese', *Cambridge Ancient History*, 2nd edn, vol. III, part 3, ch. 42, 321-59.

6. Solon of Athens

JACT (Joint Association of Classical Teachers), *The World of Athens* (Cambridge, 1984) is an introduction to Athens.

R. Meiggs, *The Athenian Empire* (Oxford: Clarendon, 1972) is detailed yet accessible.

A. Andrewes, 'The growth of the Athenian state', *Cambridge Ancient History*, 2nd edn, vol. III, part 3, ch. 43, 360-91.

Draco's law is ML no. 86, and Fornara no. 15; the text was republished by R.S. Stroud, *Drakon's Law on Homicide* (Berkeley: University of California Press, 1968). The stone is in the Epigraphic Museum of Athens; numbered *IG* i2.115+ in the corpus of Greek inscriptions.

See *Constitution of the Athenians* 2-4 for an evaluation of Draco and the early constitution of Athens.

For discussions, see Bonner and Smith 1.111-25, and MacDowell 42-3. Also M. Gagarin, *Drakon and Early Athenian Homicide Law* (New Haven, Conn: Yale University Press, 1981); E. Carawan, *Rhetoric and the Law of Draco* (Oxford: Clarendon, 1998).

Solon's laws have been collected, with German commentary, by E. Ruschenbusch, *Solonos Nomoi; ?Die fragmente des Solonischen Geseteswerkes mit einer Text- und Ueberlieferungsgeschichte* (Wiesbaden: Franz Steiner Verlag, 1983).

Biographies of Solon begin with I.M. Linforth, *Solon the Athenian* (Berkeley: University of California, 1919); K. Freeman, *The Work and Life of Solon* (Cardiff: The University of Wales Press Board, 1926; reprinted in New York: Arno Press, 1976).

Modern detailed studies of Solon's poetry include E.K. Anhalt, *Solon the Singer: Politics and Poetics* (Lanham: Rowman and Littlefield, 1993); E. Irwin, *Solon and Early Greek Poetry: The Politics of Exhortation* (Cambridge: Cambridge University Press, 2005); J. Lewis, *Solon the Thinker: Political Thought in Archaic Athens* (London: Duckworth, 2006).

7. Lesser Known Lawgivers

M. Gagarin, *Early Greek Law* discusses several lesser-known figures.

T.S. Dunbabin, *The Western Greeks* (Oxford: Oxford University Press, 1998) focuses on Italy, Sicily and the west, as does A.J. Graham, 'The

Western Greeks', *Cambridge Ancient History*, 2nd edn, vol. III, part 3, ch. 38, 163-95.

See A.J. Graham, *Colony and Mother City*, 2nd edn (Chicago Ridge: Ares, 1983) for the phenomenon of colonization.

Questions for Further Study

How do the literary treatments of various lawgivers (especially Draco, Lycurgus and Solon), by writers such as Herodotus, Aristotle, Plato, Diodorus and Plutarch compare with each other? Can their accounts be reconciled? What problems of chronology, terminology, and history do you find?

Are these writers consistent with evidence from archaic poetry? Have these writers refashioned the lawgivers in ways not consistent with that poetry? How might the terms by which the early poetry was selected for preservation by those writers influence our interpretations of the past?

How do historians, such as Herodotus, Thucydides, Polybius, and Diodorus, use the lawgivers and their laws to illustrate particular historical events? How do their treatments differ from those of biographers such as Plutarch and Diogenes Laertius?

What, given the material of archaeology and literary sources, can you infer about the lesser-known lawgivers?

How does Greek colonization – especially the *oikist,* the person selected to lead and organize the colony – relate to the figure of the lawgiver?

How did the Presocratic philosophical revolution relate to the early lawgivers? How do philosophers, such as Plato and Aristotle, use the lawgivers to support their philosophical purposes?

How far should the myths of ancient Crete be taken, in drawing inferences about early lawgivers? What are writers such as Plato, Aristotle and Polybius saying when they present Crete as a singular political entity? What of the early unification of Attica under Athens – what role might Theseus have had in this development?

How did Athenian democracy build on the reforms of Solon, and transform his legacy? Is the evidence of the fourth-century orators – especially Demosthenes – consistent with other evidence for the early lawgivers?

How did Spartan society of the fifth and fourth centuries reflect the life of Lycurgus, and is it consistent with the literary tradition associated with Lycurgus? Was his system a success, or was it doomed to failure?

How did other issues in of Greek life, such as city planning, tyranny, religious rituals, music, sculpture, vase paintings, and poetry relate to the early lawgivers, and the spread of Greek laws?

Glossary of Technical Terms

agôgê: the Spartan system of training

agôn: a contest, or a struggle, whether military, tragic, political, legal, etc.

aisumnêtês: elective, or chosen, tyranny; as Pittacus of Mytilene

aretê: excellence, or virtue

boulê: deliberative political council

dêmos: the people; as opposed to the rulers or aristocracy

dikastês: special judge on Crete

dikê: justice

ephors: Spartan officials

ethos: the 'state of mind', disposition, or habits of a person or society

eunomia: Good Order, lawfulness or the Rule of Law. From *eu* 'good' or 'well', and *nomia*, an abstract noun formed from *nomos*. This is contrasted with *dusnomia*, Bad Order, or lawlessness

helots: the enslaved Spartan serfs, especially those in Messenia

homoioi: 'Peers' or 'Equals' among the Spartan citizenry

hubris: arrogance, or outrage, and the associated assaults, esp. on the honour of another.

kosmos: an orderly arrangement or an ornament, as a city should be. Also, a political / legal official on Crete

nomos: law, or a law (*nomoi* = laws)

nomothetês: lawgiver

oikos: homestead, or home

perioikoi: The 'dwellers around' Sparta

polis: city-state (the plural is *poleis*)

politeia: political constitution; the '*polis*-ness' of the *polis*

psêphisma: a decree, esp. of the Athenian Assembly; from *psêphos* 'pebble', used in voting

rhêtôr: public speaker or orator

rhêtra: an oral statement, or an oral law; see the Spartan *Great Rhetra*

stasis: civic strife or even civil war, political unrest, factional fighting

synoikism: 'living with' or 'living together-ness'; the formation of a political union, especially used of Athens and the countryside of Attica

syssitia: common meals, practised at Crete and Sparta

themis: order; as *Themis*, a goddess in Hesiod, who bore *Eunomia,Dikê*, and *Eirênê* 'peace'

themistes: statutes, enacted by a lawgiver or body of lawgivers; similarly, *themis* was imposed by the gods

Index

Achilles, 26-7, 32-5, 39, 67
Acropolis, 64-5, 72
Aegean Sea, 49, 78, 82
Aelian, 77-81
Agamemnon, 26-8, 32, 34
Agesilaus, 61
agôgê, 59-60
agonistic culture, 15
aisumnêtês, 82
Ajax, 27-8, 32
Alcaeus, 43, 82
Amasis of Egypt, 68, 75
Androdamas of Rhegium, 76-8
Antiphon, 43
Apollo, 11, 58, 63
Apollodorus, 64
arbitration, 26-8
Archilochus, 21
Areopagus Council, 68, 72-3
aretê and excellence, 53-4, 60, 62
Aristides of Ceos, 76
Aristotle, 12, 14-15, 21, 23-4, 27, 34,
    40, 43, 46, 48-9, 54-6, 61, 64-6,
    68-9, 71-3, 76-82, 84
Arnaoutoglou, I., 44
Asia Minor, 39, 55, 57-8, 75
Athena, 11, 32, 57, 64, 77
Athens, 11-12, 14-15, 17-20, 22-4,
    27, 30, 36, 41-4, 48-53, 63-76, 79,
    83
Attica, 31, 64-5, 73
autochthonic myth, 64
axones, 72
Axus, 52

Boiotia, 77
boundary stones, 30, 69
Brasidas, 59

Carthage, 78
Catana, 14, 27, 43, 77-8
Cecrops, 64
Chalcedon, 79, 81
Chalcidice, 76-8
Charondas of Catana, 14, 26, 43, 76-9
Chios inscription, 16-17, 38
Cicero, 79
citizen, 19, 22, 27, 43, 46, 53-5, 68,
    73-4
city planning, 83-4
civil strife, 35-6, 40, 51, 68, 71, 77;
    stages of strife and resolution,
    40-2
Codrus, 64
colonies, 41-2, 55, 77-8, 50
conditional statements, 37, 45
constitution makers, opp. to
    lawgivers, 46-7, 66, 82-3
Corinth, 76, 80-1
Crete, 11-12, 18-19, 42, 44, 48-52,
    55-58, 60, 69, 75-7, 81
Croesus of Lydia, 21, 68
Croton, 78, 80
Cumae, 77
Cyclopes, 28, 30
Cylon, 51, 65
Cyme, 78
Cyprus, 75
Cyrene, 76

debts and debt slavery, 43, 67, 69,
    79; mortgages, 44-5, 69
decemvirs, 79
Deioces, 39-40
Delphi, 50-1, 55, 57-8, 63
Demades, 66
demagogues, 68
democracy, 24, 43, 58, 65, 68, 79, 84